Filming and Judgment

Filming and Judgment

Between Heidegger and Adorno

◆

Wilhelm S. Wurzer

Humanities Press International, Inc.
New Jersey ◆ London

First published 1990 by Humanities Press International, Inc.,
Atlantic Highlands, N. J., and 3 Henrietta Street, London WC2E 8LU

©Wilhelm S. Wurzer, 1990

Library of Congress Cataloging-in-Publication Data

Wurzer, Wilhelm S.
    Filming and judgment : between Heidegger and Adorno / Wilhelm
S. Wurzer.
        p.   cm. — (Philosophy and literary theory)
    Includes bibliographical references.
    ISBN 0–391–03687–4
    1. Motion pictures—Philosophy.   2. Postmodernism.
    3. Deconstruction.   4. Criticism.   I. Title.   II. Series.
PN1995.W8   1990
791.43′01–dc20   90–32366
                                                                              CIP

British Cataloguing in Publication Data

Wurzer, Wilhelm S.
    Filming and judgment : between Heidegger and Adorno. —
    (Philosophy and literary theory).
    1. Cinema films
    I. Title   II. Series
    791.43

    ISBN 0–391–03687–4

Printed in the United States of America

For
Elizabeth A. Santos

Filming and Judgment

Quicquid est, in Deo est, et nihil sine Deo esse neque concipi
potest.

Spinoza, *Ethica*

Tout est abîme, — action, désir, rêve, parole!

Baudelaire, *Les Fleurs du Mal*

Das Sein erweist sich überall hin als der Ab-grund.

Martin Heidegger, *Grundbegriffe*

Wash thine filmed eyes and look around thee.

B. Taylor, *Deukalin*

Contents

◆

Preface

◆

... I now begin
To teach you about images, so-called
A subject of most relevant importance.
These images are like a skin, a film,
Peeled from the body's surface, and they fly
This way and that way across the air; they cause
A terror in our minds, whether we wake
Or in our sleep see fearful presences.
The replicas of those who have left the light
Haunt us and startle us horribly in dreams.

Let me repeat: these images of things,
These almost airy substances, are drawn
From surfaces; you might call them film, or bark,
Something like skin, that keeps the lock, the shape
Of what it held before its wandering.

Lucretius, *De Rerum Natura*

Philosophy, suddenly, shall have awakened on a radically different site through the medium of film. Free and disenchanted, it unveils its thought, viewing a screen projecting cities of indiscernible worlds.

This book is concerned with a new awareness of philosophy's end. It is not about films. But, more importantly, it is about *filming*, a philosophical way of responding to films. Hence, it explores filming in light of a counter-metaphysical terrain in which thinking is left to wonder what thinking "itself" is still about.

For me, the *post*-aesthetic of filming first arises not only in connection with films but also out of a passage in Nietzsche's *Thus Spoke Zarathustra*, where upon hearing the words "the sign is at hand," a laughing lion shakes its head in amazement. The laughter rises above "the matter itself," the absolute, the goal, the *telos*, the essence—no longer in sight. A film of reason shatters the mirror of the viewer. Lights off, a change comes over the heart of the subject. A different view from the mountain, a new terrain, a sublime smile. Filming traces the forgotten path of imagination back to Plato's cave. There, the end of representation begins *without* the sameness of reflection. A different film returns to reason, a naming of the "death of God," the swan song of a subject casting off dialectical shields of moral ontology. More than a bedtime story, Nietzsche's vision does not let a worn-out era rest. Even in the absence of *ethos*, laughter still finds a place in thought, free to explore the narratives in films beyond the hermeneutic stage of meaning. Denoting imagination's free play with the cinematic movement of being, filming reveals the pleasure of re-marking the end of moral sameness at the turn of this century. A metonymy for the "laughing lion," filming disrupts the haunted frame of dialectical reference, while tracing the camera movements through the twists and turns of a post-cinematic judgment. The filmic text, then, is not the cinema in its immediacy, but the film as a new *distant* home for thought.

In an epoch of imaginal profusion, thinking takes on the form of filming, a post-cinematic gaze of judgment. Without anchoring thought, it points to a non-Cartesian eye *alongside* the constellation of image, music, and narrative. Beginning with the medium of film, filming ends without ending thought cinematically. It de-lights in imaging off images to clear the way for a new literature of judging (*Ur-teil*). Flowering in the strife of judgment far from the proper path to philosophy's old edifice, filming pursues different sites for thought even, and especially, in films.

What is pleasing about films, as this study will show, is not the immediacy of images per se but the challenge of discerning the representational order which continually recedes into cinematic presentations. As temporal and spatial images dissolve, the filmic pleasure of displacement surges. Filming unfolds that region of displacement in which judgment cracks the eternal wall of the absolute. Hence, filming is simply the literature of the filmic text imaging the fleeting moments of a postmodern scene. Concerned with the cinematic transfiguration of being, filming, invariably a post-Kantian operation of thought, shows that the medium of film does not remain in the condition of a cinema; instead, undesignedly, the filmic medium is transposed into a nonimaginal region of judging with unlimited narrative possibilities.

More pointedly, filming exceeds the cinematic displacement of representation in transgressing the boundaries of a free imagination without abandoning thought's relation to a tectonic of judgment. The many different sites of thinking cannot be so different from one another as not to involve the new site of judging. Filming promotes this new terrain in which the universal withdraws while the particular disperses. Discerning differently, according to a vertiginous void between Heidegger and Adorno's thinking, between being's withdrawal and identity's aesthetic diffusion, filming narrates differences emerging without the sameness of judgment.

Every effort will be made to keep the eye from being blinded by the bright surface of the Platonic sun. Without succumbing to the obscenity of imaginal excess, filming de-frames the photological images and frees thought for the laughter in judgment. To hermeneutics' distress the irony of filming's pleasure lies in judgment's release from the single, exclusive gaze of *logos*, a film whose dazzling brilliance has kept the subject watching as if the dialectic were never to end.

The essays gathered together in this volume set the tone for an unprecedented reading of judgment as filming. It is hoped that the book provides a useful focal point for continued discussion of the relationship between deconstruction, critical theory, and postmodernism while serving as a "theory" of filming, which, without simply describing the cinematographic, will shed new light on film criticism. Portions of the main text of the book are based on a much revised version of several graduate seminars taught at Duquesne University. "Nietzsche and the Problem of Ground" is an extension of an earlier paper presented at the Collegium Phaenomenologicum in Perugia, Italy, in the summer of 1988. Versions of "Postmodernism's Short Letter, Philosophy's Long Farewell" were presented at conferences of the Society for Phenomenology and Existential Philosophy in 1984 and the Heidegger Conference in 1985. Variations of these papers have been published in collected volumes of essays: *Postmodernism and Continental Philosophy*, ed. Hugh J. Silverman and Donn Welton (Albany: SUNY Press, 1988) and *Postmodernism—Philosophy and the Arts*, in *Continental Philosophy*, vol. III, ed, Hugh J. Silverman (New York and London: Routledge, 1990). The "Aesthetic Fall of Political Modernity" is an expanded version of a paper written for the 1988 meeting of the International Association for Philosophy and Literature.

In general, this project has been enriched over the years by many encounters and conversations. I am grateful to Hugh J. Silverman for encouraging me to explore the philosophical dimensions of postmodernity. I am thankful for his discerning insights into filming and for the many editorial suggestions he made toward improving my presentation.

I also stand in debt to my former colleague, John Sallis, whose work on imagination has encouraged me to pursue my project, which in part diverges significantly from his philosophy. In addition, I have benefited much from conversations with Peg Birmingham, Fred Dallmayr, Paul Davies, Barbara Freeman, Chris Fynsk, Rodolphe Gasche, Dalia Judovitz, Reginald Lilly, Cornelius Murphy, Dorothea Olkowski, Terry Pulver, Richard Rojcewicz, William Richardson, Lewis Schipper, Jose Solis-Silva, Richard Taft, Rolf VonEckartsberg, Steven Watson, Ken Westphal, David Wood, and especially Gary Shapiro. I also wish to thank my colleagues, Tom Rockmore and Andre Schuwer, for the support, stimulation, and valuable comments they have provided.

The book's inevitable flaws would have been far greater had it not been for James Quick's careful reading of each of the versions of this manuscript. I also benefited greatly from the continuous support of Judith A. Camlin of Humanities Press. Finally, I should like to thank my graduate students, notably Andrew Blasko, Mary Cavanaugh, Paul Dixon, John Giordano, Joe Good, Vanessa Howle, Robert Johnson, Paul Kinsman, Walter Lesch, Leslie Miller, Craig Peterson, Tom Urban, and Irene Wolf, friends in theoretical strife, whose comments and criticisms about general aspects of the theme of this book I could not afford to ignore.

Abbreviations

◆

The abbreviations that appear in the text, followed by page citations, refer to the following authors' works:

AT   Theodor Adorno, *Aesthetic Theory*, trans. C. Lenhardt (London and New York: Routledge & Kegan Paul, 1984)

BGE   Friedrich Nietzsche, *Beyond Good and Evil*, trans. W. Kaufmann (New York: Random House, Inc., 1966)

BW   Martin Heidegger, *Basic Writings*, trans. D. F. Krell (New York: Harper & Row, 1977)

CJ   Immanuel Kant, *Critique of Judgment*, trans. W. S. Pluhar (Indianapolis: Hackett Publishing Co., 1987)

CR   Immanuel Kant, *Critique of Pure Reason*, trans N. K. Smith (New York: St. Martin's Press, 1965)

D   Jacques Derrida, *Dissemination*, trans. B. Johnson (Chicago: University of Chicago Press, 1981)

ED   Martin Heidegger, *Aus der Erfahrung des Denkens (1910–1976)* (Frankfurt am Main: Vittorio Klostermann, 1983)

FM   Charles Baudelaire, *Les Fleurs du Mal*, trans. R. Howard (Boston: David R. Godine, 1983)

GM   Friedrich Nietzsche, *On the Genealogy of Morals*, trans. W. Kaufmann and R. J. Hollingdale (New York: Vintage Books, 1969)

HCT   Martin Heidegger, *History of the Concept of Time*, trans. T. Kisiel (Bloomington: Indiana University Press, 1985)

M   Jacques Derrida, *Margins of Philosophy*, trans. A. Bass (Chicago: University of Chicago Press, 1982)

OG   Jacques Derrida, *Of Grammatology*, trans. G. C. Spivak (Baltimore: Johns Hopkins University Press, 1976)

OT   Michel Foucault, *The Order of Things*, trans. A. Sheridan-Smith (New York: Random House, Inc., 1970)

P   Theodor Adorno, *Prisms*, trans. S. and S. Weber (Cambridge, Mass.: The MIT Press, 1981)

PF   Friedrich Hölderlin, *Poems and Fragments*, trans. M. Hamburger (Ann Arbor: The University of Michigan Press, 1968).

Po   Jacques Derrida, *Positions*, trans. A. Bass (Chicago: University of Chicago Press, 1981)

PS   Arthur Kroker and David Cook, *The Postmodern Scene* (New York: St. Martin's Press, 1986)

QT   Martin Heidegger, *The Question Concerning Technology and Other Essays*, trans. W. Lovitt (New York: Harper & Row, 1977)

S   John Sallis, *Spacings—of Reason and Imagination* (Chicago: University of Chicago Press, 1987)

Se   Martin Heidegger, *Seminare, Gesamtausgabe*, Vol. 15 (Frankfurt am Main: Vittorio Klostermann, 1986)

SZ   Martin Heidegger, *Sein und Zeit* (Tübingen, Max Niemeyer, 1967)

TK   Martin Heidegger, *Die Technik und die Kehre* (Tübingen: Verlag Gunther Neske, 1962)

TM   Rodolphe Gasché, *The Tain of the Mirror* (Cambridge Mass.: Harvard University Press, 1986)

WG   Martin Heidegger, "Vom Wesen des Grundes," in *Wegmarken* (Frankfurt am Main: Vittorio Klostermann, 1976)

Introduction
Filming the Pale Cast
of 'Mimesis'

As images of the twentieth century fade into a silent *promesse du bonheur*, philosophy is prepared to explore a new beginning. Deflecting from the principle of ground, it will show itself differently as it advances toward a site that exceeds political, moral, and social spacings. In the wake of this challenge, philosophy greets the turn of this century without rushing to essences, without compelling theories to yield to praxeological strategies. Ironically, however, metaphysics continues to flourish at the beginning of its end. Whence it is not surprising that metaphysics endures in technology, while the principle of ground as the metaphysical concept *par excellence* is radically questioned in the human sciences. Indeed, in the social order of things, metaphysics has become what it always had been in the proto-Platonic realm of ideas: a systematic "concealing" of being, a dialectical self-justification of power. Now, disengaged from theory, the principle of ground prevails in a praxis of enframing (*Ge-stell*),[1] discerned in a systematic consolidation of the technical and dialectical. As a result of this socio-technical presencing of reason, a placid functionalism persists even in legal and ethico-political judgments. If principles which determine such judgments are scarcely ever questioned in accordance with the sustained metaphysical power of the *principium rationis sufficientis*, today's increasingly complex discourse on "the order of things" merely reflects the debility of fading propositions. In a world in which praxis resists thought, and theorizing appears to be no more than praxeological comfort, the irony of *mimesis* lies in the eternal return of the same old reflections. A double-edged sword thus shines at the abyss of this epoch: *images* of practical grounding without theoretical legitimation collide with a *style of thinking* which, withdrawing from ground, is drawn into this very withdrawal.

Beyond an explicit or implicit political agenda in a post-Cartesian manner of radical doubt, thinking reveals an open texture of transformative possibilities. While disrupting the foundational assumptions of a social hermeneutics, thinking does not espouse disjunctive sets of cultural simulation. With a scope of vision not unrelated to what Kant calls "the free lawfulness of imagination," it responds to the epochal paradox of a withering of the metaphysical subject *and* the rise of an expressive computerization of representation. Accordingly, in its radical turn to a post-essentialist manner of judging, thinking "can neither plant [its] feet on the bottom nor swim on the surface."[2] Dismantling the principle of ground *and* the illusion of groundlessness, it grants a "different beginning": an unforeseeably new site for judgment, pointing at once to the rupture in metaphysics without imposing a metaphysical script.[3]

This "other beginning" does not shelter thinking with political, social, or aesthetic awnings. Instead, it invites thought to break out of the interdependence of metaphysics and technology, and by finer than dialectic means it reveals a manner of judging in relation to the dispersions of a post-aesthetic site of imagination. Eliding the limitations of illusion and truth, thinking asserts its connection to the paradoxical situation in which judgment finds "itself" as it faces the gulf that separates a "principled" technology from the sheer force of an unprincipled humanity. Images of ground colliding with feelings of groundlessness highlight an unbreakable connection between an illusion of order and the truth of its narrowly framed interests.

Filming and Judgment seeks to respond to the paradox of judgment's post-essentialist disarray. The following text is especially concerned with the question of an anticipated collapse of the principle of ground in the epochal terrain of judgment, a scene which I shall call *filming*. Filming, then, is the name for a new site of judgment at the turn of the century. Its name, initially derived from the Old English words *filmen* and *felling*, has no metaphysical history per se. And yet, without being called by its current name, a trace of it can already be discerned in Plato's notion of *eidos*, a being that shines prior to all images.[4] Indeed, the entire history of metaphysics can be viewed as a genealogy of "filming" in which reason "films" the ground of all beings. Confronting the "corrective hypothesis" of western metaphysics (*homoiosis*), for the most part, the dialectic which serves to show being its truth, filming signifies a manner of thinking which uncovers a narrow showing or "filming" of being that hinges on the metaphysical presumptions of a definite ground.[5] Filming thus deconstructs the dialectic empire in the genealogy of metaphysics. One can venture to say that it emerges in a philosophical discourse for which judgment is no longer under the spell of the identity of reason and ground, and in a time when judgment (*Ur-teil*) moves forward to a radically different terrain.[6] To that end, filming begins to think what metaphysics leaves unthought—judgment's *Ab-grund* in relation to imagination.[7]

Still, exceeding the dialectic meaning of imagination, filming serves to show what happens in judgment even "beyond" Kant's concept of imaginal "free play" in the *Critique of Judgment*. In dismantling the sovereignty of images in theory and cultural praxis, filming signifies more than what imagination *more metaphysico* represents. It cannot be read as a conventional mapping of *Einbildungskraft* in which the principle of subsumption, by means of which the particular is reconciled with the universal, determines the power of judgment. Free of the transcendental structures determining the predicative unity of appearances and the thing in itself, judgment, in a radical withdrawal from Kant's metaphysical vestige of purposiveness, cultivates a post-aesthetic space named filming. Facing the abyss, filming manifests the sublime and vertiginous turns and twists of judgment in the postmodern scene of imagination's excessive possibilities. But as these possibilities disengage thought from the presence of being, filming, at the limit of *Ereignis*, is no longer wedded to a discourse on truth. From a metaphysical perspective, it is judgment gone astray; from the viewpoint of a new style of thought, it is judgment discerning its freedom.

In a sublime straying, filming provides no place of repose, withdrawing not only from a metaphysical "filming" of being but also from a cinematographic extension of *logos*. Diverging from a dialectic which continues to speak metaphysically in the very discourse of the cinema, filming disrupts the theoretical and practical movements of *logos*, no less important to the formation of films per se. Clearly, in our text, filming does not rest upon a dialectic or cinematographic sense of "filming." In what follows, that which will be rendered as consonant with a manner of judging will be radically different from a dialectical, technical determination of judgment (*Urteilskraft*). Thus, provided filming is taken into account at the very edge of the margins of imagination, it is manifestly philosophical for several reasons. First, it challenges the metaphysics of "filming," i.e., a dialectic appropriation of being in which a logocentric "film" darkens the very shining of being while judgment is anchored in the self-presence of *eidos*. Second, filming enables thinking to break free of the "film" or absolute coating of reason. Third, prompted by Kant's *Critique of Judgment*, filming exhibits a different manner of judging, a *Beurteilung*—an imaginal mode of discerning which releases imagination toward radical disinterestedness. Exceeding the polarities of ground and surface, truth and illusion, there is a sense in which filming emerges as "the disinterested relation" of relations, illustrating imaginations's fall from the principle of *telos*.

Within this context, we shall also focus on a philosophical reading of the imaginal terrain of an epoch paradoxically related to the "intercultural" movements of cinematic images. Cavell, Deleuze, Rentschler, Rothman, and others have clearly demonstrated the importance of the cinematic in relation to our understanding of being.[8] Arguably, films can now be studied as instances of philosophical texts founded not on metaphysical discourse but on a distinctly appreciative constellation of image, music, and language. Within this constellation, filming is invariably open to judgment's disruptive twists and turns. By the same token, filming can be taken as a modality of judging what certain film directors strive to achieve in films. Without developing a theory of filming as such, Werner Herzog, for one, regards filmmaking as a cinematic itinerary of thought in search of the sublime.[9] For him, film, an imaginal artform, which bounces images off each other and against each other, advances a manner of judging that is not determined by images. More closely considered, the irony of filming can be said to lie in a possible disappearance of images so that the highlighting of the art of language in films may exceed the cinematic structure of any particular film. The unlimited possibilities of filming are continually intertwined with the event of imaginal withdrawal in judgment's free play with disinterestedness. The matter of filming is seldom so simple as to be connected merely with filmmaking. Indeed, at every level of *Beurteilung*, filming notices what the eye cannot see in the myriad movement of images. For this reason, filming always already precedes a series of visions we call "cinema."

Beyond the rhetoric of the visual, filming concurs with an implosive sighting of postmodern *Zerissenheit*,[10] a strife that comes on the scene in a time without *Geist*. The slashing of *Zeitgeist*, far from signifying a dissonant nihilism, ushers in an "understanding" of judgment which springs from a filmic fissuring of ground and groundlessness. While showing no dialectic concern for presence and absence, otherness and sameness, filming frees thinking from a received dialectic adherence to either position or negation. In effect, filming is the *sight/site* of a disjunction of judgment (*Ur-teil*) as reason is radically displaced. Transgressing the phenomenal and noumenal domains of a critical philosophy, filming marks a new comportment toward world, an imaginal de-sighting of being which distinguishes "our time" from previous historical epochs.

Related to *phainesthai*,[11] filming is indicative of a modern age whose "essence" lies precisely in *Kehre*, a technical turn *in* being to a singular way of apprehending things. "To be new," Heidegger writes, "is peculiar to the world that has become image" (*QT*, 132). The transformation of world into an imaginal domain, simultaneously technical and aesthetic, begins with the dominance of a filmic representation of beings which radically modifies the form of human presence. Yet, while appearing to suggest an imaginal control over beings, filming disrupts the mediation of things through images in modes of judging which ostensibly exceed cinematic avenues of meaning.

Furthermore, the *phainesthai* that emerges in filming is a "showing" no longer charged with ontology. On the contrary, what is seen now is judgment without the "primordial itself," free for a post-aesthetic of filming.

But what does it mean to pose the question of filming with regard to a post-aesthetic? Without claiming to exhaust the matter of filming in a "philosophic," post-aesthetic sense, this text traces a unique manner of judging to what thinking is yet to be. What is expected of thinking with regard to filming is perhaps quite different from what philosophy expects of reflection. There is no anticipation of being, truth, or *telos* in filming. Indeed, one could say that filming takes (*capere*) precisely the metaphysical anticipation out of thinking in anticipation of thinking's ability to be in a radically different space, an unknown luminous distance from ground. In all questions involving filming, therefore, a post-aesthetic necessitates a singularity of judgment which dissolves the imaginal *telos* without abandoning the filmic *kinesis* of thinking. Exceeding appearance and essence, filming can be described variously as an evanescent, ruptured movement of "spirit" without originary unity or purpose, invariably disrupting the epistemic ground of the dialectic as well as the ontologic interplay of presence and absence. As post-aesthetic, filming erases what is teleological in a genealogy of the aesthetic. Still, the matter of its judging (*Ur-teil*) remains "aesthetic" insofar as the question of art is explored within a postmodern site of thinking. In turn, filming reveals the dimension of art in thought, a judgment (*Ur-teil*) open to filmic possibilities, namely, what is yet to be (seen). While it is absurd to render thinking as art, in "an other beginning" thinking may manifest expressly what is unique in filming: a manner of judging that seeks the beautiful without a "metaphysical" vision. Ironically, the beautiful in a post-aesthetic sense is what is yet to be, a "different beginning." Such a beginning is always already "anticipated" in judging the filmic constellation of image, music, and discourse. A post-aesthetic of filming, then, disrupts the alliance of reflection and aesthetics, i.e., the subjectivity of aesthetic reflection. A poetic rupturing of *Ur-teil* brings to view the open strife of a pure work of art, imagination dislodging *Ur* from *teil*, unfolding judgment's unimaginable route to an "anti-art" of disinterestedness. Falling from philosophical essentiality (*Ur*), judgment surges freely as a postmodern link (*teil*) in the sublime chain of difference.

While questions of origin and teleology remain problematic for a post-aesthetic of filming, the concept of "disinterestedness," when it does not yield to a flowering of moral taste, is singularly important. Indeed, filming marks the utter radicality of disinterestedness, continually opening judgment to the collisions, frictions, and dissonances of imaginal relations. Not bound to essential structures, filming reveals a strife (*Zerissenheit*) in judgment, a disinterested opening in which time and spirit (*Zeitgeist*) fall from identity, concealing a thinking yet to be. In its post-aesthetic radicality, filming sways between *Ereignis* and a "different beginning," between Heidegger and Adorno's naming of thought, deflecting from the mirror of truth while judging a non-mimetic play of free relations.

A tripartite coating films our genealogy of filming: one, the exceedingly dialectical coating that arises in the power of *logos* linked to the representational dominance of "an abiding and unchanging I";[12] two, the felling of this coating in filming in the disinterested mode of radical judging; three, the filming in "filmmaking" which dissolves the imaginal and frees judgment for what is yet to be (seen).

To that end, *Filming and Judgment* crystallizes a new turn in the postmodern progression of thought by deconstructing the power of "image appropriations." Questioning the use and abuse of imagination, the text examines filming's radical alternative to the hegemony of an "image-oriented" reflection. To expose the filmic task of thinking, this investigation is divided into three parts.

A genealogical background for a theory of filming is provided in Part I, which focuses upon certain texts of Nietzsche, Heidegger, and Foucault. First, Nietzsche's work is situated with regard to the philosophical problem of ground. His thought is shown to reveal an aesthetic phenomenalism in which a radical deepening anticipates a singular sense of filming. Without naming filming as such, Nietzsche develops an "imaginal willing" which is nonetheless confined to an ontological expansion of the concept of the will to power.

In further exploring the complexity of filming, Heidegger's thought is examined in relation to a postmodern disruption of imagination. His decisive insights into world as imaginal phenomenon are pursued in a manner which eventually exceeds what he understood himself to say. Thus, while the notion of filming is initially incumbent upon an understanding of *phainesthai*, which with its ways of showing does not center in *ratio* but is carried away toward "dis-positions" of *Gelassenheit*, it diverges from the ontological development of Heidegger's thought.[13]

Part I concludes with an *entracte* in the discussion on filming in which Foucault's critical reading of Velázquez's aesthetic decentering of ground is reviewed in order to reveal the ironic interplay of modernity and postmodernism within a countermetaphysical order of representation. This section highlights the difficulty of withdrawing from the reflexivity of metaphysics.

Accordingly, Part II explores Adorno's critique of pure *mimesis* in light of our inquiry into filming. His text, *Aesthetic Theory*, is viewed as evidencing imagination's transition from modernity to postmodernism. An enhanced imaginal terrain of judgment revealed in Adorno's aesthetic genealogy indicates that thinking begins anew in attending to a redemptive "apparitional" power of art. As effacement of "filming" or dialectical imaging, filming is in part related to Adorno's aesthetic delineation of "apparition." While the term "apparition" is chosen to designate filming's radical fall from the principle of ground (indeed, from all epistemology of essencing), it is also, undesignedly, brought into relation with a postmodern perceptibility of capital.

What follows demonstrates that Adorno's reflections on art signify an aesthetic fall of modernity, thus ushering in the end of a marxian *mimesis*. Arguably, however, Adorno's own imaginal limitations of a horizontal *mimesis* introduce an antinomy which consists in the illusion of reinscribing presence from a modernist (marxist) perspective into a seemingly subversive aesthetic delimitation of ground. The text will demonstrate that a nonimaginal showing such as filming exceeds Adorno's dialectically open *mimesis* as well as Heidegger's ontologically bound view of imitation.

Part II ends with a reading of Kant's *Critique of Judgment* as a text that not only precedes the theme of filming in Nietzsche, Heidegger, and Foucault, but that is also already en route to the aesthetic disruptions of judgment in Adorno's philosophy. Deeply entangled in disinterestedness, reflective judgment is shown to diverge from the metaphysical script of representation, while exposing the philosophical thrust of a new epistemic turn to a possible pure work of art in relation to the poetic supplementarity of Hölderlin and Baudelaire.

Part III expands the notion of filming and explores its implications with regard to the crisis of imagination and a seemingly postmodern aperture of judgment. The text reveals how filming dismantles subjectivity, particularly the narrow operations of an epistemology determined by teleology and essentiality. It sketches an itinerary of filming from imaginal "free play" to radical spacings of judgment. On this view, filming is envisioned as part of a process which releases imagination from teleologic anchorings for a distinctive opening or strife which makes judgment (*Ur-teil*) operative in relation to capital, now regarded as breaking the mirror of *mimesis*. This study, therefore, inaugurates a reading of capital that opens an epoch, beyond the power of production, to a filming which judges freely. It also advances the thought that a nonessentialist mode of judging manifests capital without channelling the latter into a "positive" or "negative" reading of an epoch. Accordingly, judgment "functions" in filming without being bound to finality, yet linked to what metaphysics seems to have left unthought, a com-posed rather than a received notion of capital. It shall be noted, however, that capital is not the name for money or what Schopenhauer calls "human happiness *in abstracto*," but rather a name for what cannot be named in filming, indeed for what cannot be grounded in the groundlessness of an epoch. Capital shines forth as sight of the siteless, as apparition of ground, as beauty of pure filming. Part III concludes by extending even further than earlier discussions the notion of filming as a mode of judging peculiar to the *Zerissenheit* of this epoch. While it shows filming's affinity with contemporary deconstructive theories, it also directs a confrontation with the thought of Heidegger and Derrida.

What begins as an effort to unfold filming as a contemporary philosophical *Blicksprung*[14] and a postmodern discourse on capital ends with a brief glance at a modality of filming operative in the cinematic strategies of such filmmakers as Herzog, Fassbinder, and Hitchcock. The exergue to this text offers an *entre* of filming and "filming"—a *filmen*, an imaginal attempt at presenting what cannot be "represented" in a "filming" or coating of reality through metaphysics and through the teleologic mode of Hollywood "filming." *Filmen* is not yet filming; still, it is the beginning of "brightness playing,"[15] of judgment moving in the open so that Auschwitz will not be filmed again.

Part One

◆

IMAGINAL DELIMITATIONS

1

◆

Nietzsche and the Problem of Ground

The history of metaphysics has largely been guided by what Leibniz calls "the grand principle" of ground, whose concise formula states: "Nihil est sine ratione." Nothing is without reason or ground, without ultimate explanation, without the certitude of dialectic presence. Moreover, the principle of ground signifies a system of concepts, a totality of connected ideas in a unique dialectic terrain that consolidates reason and ground. This peculiar but certain oneness is first and foremost radically questioned by Nietzsche. Indeed, one of the important aims of his philosophy is the undoing of the metaphysical identity of *Vernunft* and *Grund*. Thus, his inscription of difference in aesthetic configurations marks a significant attempt at dismantling the principle of sufficient reason.

Accordingly, in what follows I will first outline Nietzsche's attempts at transforming the principle of sufficient reason set in motion in the *Birth of Tragedy* and *Thus Spoke Zarathustra*. I then direct my attention to the very process of Nietzsche's subversion of ground as it culminates in the *Genealogy of Morals* and in *The Twilight of the Idols*, particularly in relation to his observations on the political. In retrospect, I will ask whether Nietzsche's withdrawal from ground unveils an antifoundationalist mode of thought or whether it is merely a digression which serves the traditional principle of ground anew.

REASON'S DIONYSIAN SITE

Early in his philosophy Nietzsche recognizes that the problem of ground is intimately connected with the question of reason. His aesthetic projection of the primal One (*das Ureine*) shows that ground and cause have been mistakenly aligned in the history of metaphysics. He claims that one can conceive *das Ureine* as ground of all things without granting pertinence to the idea of ground as *causa*, or even as *causa rationis*. In effect, the very idea of cause, at least in its conventional cause-effect connection, becomes problematic in *The Birth of Tragedy*. Ground as primal One is too dynamic, complex, and conflictual to be the simple, absolute cause of appearances. Initially, therefore, Nietzsche sees the problem of ground not merely as one of separating cause from ground but, more importantly, as one of reason's withdrawal from ground. Thus, Nietzsche's aesthetic genealogy radically transforms the principle of sufficient reason by dissolving the logocentric identity of reason and ground. *The Birth of Tragedy* begins this process by granting imagination the Apollinian freedom of standing outside reason's estranged dialectical self-presence. It sets up a new world for reason, a different ground sustained by a Dionysian perspective of suffering. This transformative view of ground seeks to express reason's tragic spacings in relation to reality rather than to "pure" reason. Nietzsche, therefore, accounts for reason-in-reality, reason-in-nature, reason as Dionysian phenomenon. The idea of ground is reinscribed, but not as pure cause or reason. Ground is now *other* than reason as "reason." This radical other is the aesthetic phenomenon of reason turning to difference, to imagination, far from the metaphysical region where reason and ground are one and the same.

A closer look at the matter of reason in *The Birth of Tragedy* shows that reason is aesthetically grounded in the metaphysical abyss of the primal One, *das Ureine*, the absolute imaginal space of pain and contradiction. Torn between the Apollinian desire to be free from primordiality and the ironic Dionysian impulse expressive of the primal One, reason, in a new face which Nietzsche calls "a discursive image" (*eine Bilderrede*),[1] reveals the aesthetic tensions of the beautiful and the sublime. This "discursive image" marks a dissemination of ground whose perspective of imaginal identity signifies an aesthetic, albeit metaphysical, opening for difference. The difference of ground and reason becomes particularly operative in the Apollinian-Dionysian interplay of image and power. In turn, reason's *Bilderrede* is more than a discourse on the image of the Apollinian-Dionysian constellation; it is a discourse on primal desire conceived as reason desiring to exceed the appearances of the primal One. On this view, a tragic showing begins to challenge the Socratic dialectic seductively aligned with morality. Reason is seen as *das Ureine* extending its power over a terrain of thought which exceeds the moral and political boundaries of Socrates' search for truth. This tragic movement of reason about the center of an aesthetic ground points to a Dionysian revolution of reason, a disclosive art of thinking beyond the haunting terrain of consciousness. Still, consciousness plays a role in this drama of reason. While the Dionysian impulse encumbers the dialectic spirit of consciousness, in the Apollinian instance of individuation, consciousness turns its probing eyes toward images of the beautiful.

Accordingly, *The Birth of Tragedy* reveals a dehiscence of reason, an aesthetic difference within the primal territory of imaginal identity. Dislodged from the Socratic dialectic for which it had only existed as a pure object of reflection, reason is now free to discern its falling. Nietzsche's early philosophy, therefore, betokens the event of reason's fall from the proprietary essence of ground to the aesthetic abyss of imagination. In *Oedipus Rex*, Creon's advice to Oedipus may serve to show this paradoxical turn: "Crave not to be master of all things: for the mastery which you had won, has not followed you through life."[2]

The Birth of Tragedy takes up the challenge of Sophocles' notion of reason as a displaced, abandoned phenomenon in search of truth. It tells the uncanny tale of reason's new adventure. No longer master of being, reason unfolds slowly, ironically, from one mode of reflection to the next, without yielding to the dialectical desire for an illusory repose. For Nietzsche, reason, disengaged from its former dreams, emerges as *parodos* (*paradein*— "to sing more") of truth, the first appearance of the chorus of tragic reflection. As *parodos*, reason, in a powerful aesthetic extension of the primal One, plays out the parody of imaginal identity. Entering the stage of Dionysian *lethe* or primordial forgetfulness, reason sings of a new ground, an aesthetic chaos, far from the Hegelian retreat of *Geist*. Gliding over Hegelian transitions without falling to the ground, reason strikes out against the scowling, teleo-logocentric eyes of "consciousness." An aesthetic approximation of the tragic act of Oedipus grants free space for reason. Its discourse penetrates the parodic Dionysian site of imagination: "Why was I to see, when sight could show me nothing sweet?"[3] The mirror of dialectical reflection had merely shown a hermeneutic process of subduing the natural, of controlling what is real, of linking being to a logical goal "by the shortest route and with the smallest expenditure of force,"[4] at the expense of imagination.

REASON'S IMAGINAL DEHISCENCE

The tragic, aesthetic displeasure with metaphysics' seeing, with the historic unfolding of a logocentric ground, is enhanced by Nietzsche's revolutionary invitation to disharmonize the Socratic dialectic. Apollo's image of reason's flight from ground projects a new mode of seeing, a filming in the manner of a "parodic" Dionysian turn to the aesthetic abyss of the primal One. Granted, reason is not yet free from *arche*. The Dionysian turn to art's origin, which makes possible the birth of tragic thought, is still committed to a principle of ground. Nevertheless, for a brief moment in the Apollinian spacings of *The Birth of Tragedy*, reason is free for the imaginal production of appearances receding from ground. Attaining a certain moment (*Augenblick*) of freedom in *Thus Spoke Zarathustra*, reason, in general, however, is either preceded by a tragic Dionysian sense of oneness in the early works, or by the will to power as essential principle in the later works. This does not mean that there are no traces of withdrawal from ground in Nietzsche's works. There are, indeed, signs of radical attempts to overturn the principle of ground in *Thus Spoke Zarathustra*. One might even argue that Nietzsche is often creatively engaged in deconstructing a metaphysics of presence.[5] But as we shall see, his genealogy, which is still caught up in the *language* of metaphysics, is primarily a critique of classical ontology and does not exceed the aesthetic-political essence of ground. At most, his genealogy anticipates a radically different space of reason, imagination's postdialectic dehiscence.

Such anticipation can be discerned in the form of a metaphysical play in *Thus Spoke Zarathustra*. There, the event of "the death of God" is initially reason's decisive attempt to recapture the Apollinian moment of freedom. The image of Dionysos is significant but only in relation to Zarathustra's subversive (Apollinian) discourse. The idea of an Apollinian-Dionysian constellation with its differentiated amplitude is no longer determined by a primal-ground. Instead, it is enshrined in an ontotheologic absence of ground. Zarathustra appears as "moving image" of reason, as the "fluid element" of tragic reflection.[6] What concerns us here is precisely a discourse in which reason is engaged in a certain play of imagination free of the absolute.[7] *Thus Spoke Zarathustra* advances a new kind of identity between imagination and reason, one in which reason is no longer granted an ontologic privilege over imagination. Nevertheless, in spite of reason's imaginal dehiscence, it is still sheltered by the eternal wills to power. While there may be infinite interpretations, they are invariably interpretations of power.

This leads to the central question concerning Nietzsche's text: Is power as will radically different from the principle of ground? That it varies from the aesthetic ground of the *Birth of Tragedy* can be seen from Nietzsche's consideration of the ultimate fall of the absolute in *Thus Spoke Zarathustra*. But how else does will to power as principle of the revaluation of all values differ from the traditional principle of ground? For one, will to power recedes from the absolute ontology of the principle of sufficient reason. This operation illustrates that ground is no longer conceived of as being. And yet, Nietzsche still thinks of ground as *Wesen*; indeed, the will to power is the *essence* of truth. Nietzsche's compulsion toward the thought of the eternal return of the wills to power indicates an epistemic betrayal of an earlier, subversive mode of thought. The Apollinian desire to be free from ground, which for a brief moment outwits all manner of dialectics, is now entirely repressed by a new metaphysical play of power revealed in *Thus Spoke*

Zarathustra. Dionysos, who signifies the unity of man and the primal One, is faintly present in this play. He no longer resembles the image of *The Birth of Tragedy* with its "gospel of universal harmony." Exceeding the aesthetic, metaphysical dimension of the primal One, the new principle of power disengages reason from tragic unity. What emerges now is a genealogical play of forces, the wills to power *sub specie aeternitatis*. This exclusive Apollinian orientation is clearly evident throughout *Thus Spoke Zarathustra*. From the moment that Zarathustra fails to communicate his thought on a socio-metaphysical level, the image of ground appears as power of individuation. An intriguing transition occurs in the text. Zarathustra's discourse exhibits an aesthetic *Kehre*: the image of Dionysos becomes the face of Apollo beyond the primal One and the emancipatory concerns of *The Birth of Tragedy*. Whence it is not surprising that in *Thus Spoke Zarathustra*, the story of the "death of God" is no more than a fable of Apollo's beautiful "metaphysical" illusion—the eternal wills to power.

A New Economy of Presence

The *Genealogy of Morals* calls for an active forgetting of being, for an opening of reason that will enable it to break away from a consciousness with a moral complicity of contrary values. One may think of Nietzsche's genealogy as an art of enactment, a strategy of dissension which critically dismantles morality's "sense-less" indebtedness to dialectic. Its critique of subjectivity radically questions the value of a dialectic ground operative in moral ontology. But even as an art of critique, genealogy is not entirely free from a substantive creditor. Ironically, this creditor will surface in the pluralized spaces of reason's genealogy, so that the configurations of reason and imagination are not able to assert themselves outside the digressive but solid space of the wills to power. Nietzsche's principle of power, therefore, announces essence without essence-appearance distinctions. This means, of course, that there is still a metaphysical eye inspecting the spacings of reason. Imagination and reason are still in commerce with a power whose very presence constitutes a new debt for reason. Genealogy's slippage into the open simultaneously limits reason's "free play" to the "latest and noblest form" of the ascetic ideal, the wills to power. Guided by this non-derivative concept, Nietzsche's genealogy assigns limitations to a deconstruction of presence. Reflection is reduced to the plane of power-quanta which do not appear to be empirical or transcendental signifieds but are still inscribed under the rubric of essence. It is true that the post-dialectical wills to power emerge as detours of a radically new presence, as moments in the interval of essence and appearance, as forces of an uncanny space somewhere between individuation and ground, between Apollo and Dionysos, between reason and imagination. Nevertheless, the process of reason's emancipation from philosophical essentiality is halted by a new essence, a new economy of higher principles, the political ontology of the wills to power. No doubt, Nietzsche's text challenges reason's confinement to dialectical presence, but can it account for reason's occlusion, its "final spacing,"[8] its seemingly indemnifying debt to the eternal return of the wills to power? Despite its polythematic positions, Nietzsche's critical genealogy always seems to circle back to the principle of power. Indeed, the text consistently asks, How far can reason reach into the essence of power? Thus, the problem of ground begins anew with this text. And the *Genealogy of Morals* fails to think without a nostalgia for ground.

THE AESTHETIC AMBIGUITY OF 'GREAT POLITICS'

The essentialist mood of Nietzsche's philosophy of the will to power is enhanced by frequent allusions to such cultural master concepts as "the strongest souls of today," "men of great creativity," "higher men," "dominating and Caesarian spirits," "masters of the earth," and so forth. These utterances evoke a renewed interest in extending the principle of ground toward individuation, toward an Apollinian image of a new political order. Even though Nietzsche takes into account the twilight of truth, his critique of metaphysics paves the way for a new grounding, an anchoring of "great politics." The "beautiful illusion" of the Apollinian image develops into Nietzsche's own illusion of the "beautiful form" of "great human beings." It should therefore be asked: Do we encounter something new in Nietzsche's *Kehre* to the political terrain?

What is philosophically fruitful about his unique ontological elevation of the individual—this creative, rational human being who invariably stands above and against the ordinary man? What are we to make of his attempts to lodge the political order of rank in the sphere of Apollinian imagination? How are we to understand Nietzsche's "new, tremendous aristocracy, based on the severest self-legislation, in which the will of philosophical men of power and artist-tyrants will be made to endure for millennia"?[9] It is quite clear that the *Kehre* from the twilight of truth to a "new enlightenment" of reason announces a time whose politics will have a different meaning.[10] This meaning, however, is not clarified by Nietzsche. Indeed, there is no explanatory social theory in Nietzsche's philosophy. This apparent lack of theoretical clarity does not diminish Nietzsche's emphasis on a new economy of political ontology. The will to power is advanced as a historical concept, indeed, as a socio-political category. In the summer of 1888, Nietzsche writes: "The will to power as life: high point of historical self-consciousness."[11] It is not our purpose here to reinscribe a hermeneutic gesture in Nietzsche's text. It is there already, notably, in the very irony of his formidable *Kehre*, in the political image of *Gestaltlosigkeit* ("formlessness"), in Nietzsche's final indelible image of exclusivity. Despite the genealogical dehiscence of reason, the image of the political order becomes thematically distinct: "great human beings," "breeding," "order of rank," "the strong of the future," "the masters of the earth." Is Nietzsche's irrepressible desire for political presence an attempt to assimilate Hegel's and Fichte's construction of history? Can we speak here of Nietzsche's classic (Dionysian) political metaphysics?

No doubt, Nietzsche radicalizes the metaphysical concept of ground in his corpus as a whole. He profoundly changes the direction of philosophical thought up to his time. But, notwithstanding all the productive instances of his thought, we must ask why a great portion of his thought, particularly the last phase, is so concerned with activating a new political diction of breeding and cultivating "order of rank." If "will to power" is really the "high point of historical self-consciousness," does this signify the completion of the Western teleological ideal? Like metaphysicians before him, Nietzsche is still preoccupied with the last and highest totality of things. His principle of the will to power does not provide us with theme-effects capable of disengaging thought from all dialecticity; rather, it provides us with a thematic nucleus which merely interrupts or suspends the classical equation of reason and ground. In turn, the image of the overman does not undo metaphysics in any radical sense; it rejuvenates the history of thought in "the grand style" of *gaya scienza*, the blithe science of a new political order. In *Ecce Homo* Nietzsche writes: "It is only beginning with me that the earth knows *grosse Politik*."[12] Metaphysics is now explored as an all-embracing historical science. Of course, Nietzsche's compulsion to large-scale politics does not reflect the petty political situation of Bismarckian Germany, but rather a genuine spiritual confrontation (*Auseinandersetzung*) with the governments of his time. *Great politics* entails the science of "new philosophers," "legislators of the future." As such, its metaphysics is a science of the "wills to power," which is neither a transcendental nor a deconstructive theory of the political order. Still, as a new system of values it is committed to the principle of ground. The image of individuation, which culminates in Zarathustra's philosophy of the overman, is a mere "photograph" of the concept of the will to power. To that end, Nietzsche's image of "great politics" does not seem to move outside of a metaphysical terrain. Enshrined in the "beautiful illusion" of power, the seemingly new political image remains frozen. The irony of Nietzsche's political judgment lies in his own admission: "My consolation is that everything that has been is eternal."[13]

Does this thought invite the possibility of a new political theory of ground? Undoubtedly, Nietzsche's preoccupation with the question of a new economy of "higher culture" does not advance his "radical hermeneutics" of infinite interpretations. Attempts to "assassinate two millennia of antinature" seem to fail in light of his strong Apollinian desire to legitimate "great politics." Even his renunciation of the concept of being becomes problematic with his new "will to power" conception of the world. Thus, the political turn to "the masters of the earth" is merely an elegant reconstitution of the ideal Renaissance man. Elements of Nietzsche's intense adherence to an *Übermensch* society can be discerned in Jakob Burckhardt's study of the Italian Renaissance. Accordingly, at least two questions arise: Are the future masters of the earth slaves of the past? Is Nietzsche's philosophy of power merely the eternal return of monumental history?

IMAGINAL CONSTELLATIONS

In order to respond to these questions, it is necessary to clarify some critical aspects of Nietzsche's aesthetic transformation of the principle of ground. For one, the principle of ground as reason is transformed into a principle of ground as will to power. This radical displacement of reason reveals ground as image, more adequately, as "world of images" (*Welt der Bilder*),[14] that is, as constellation of the aesthetic and the political. Thinking, therefore, no longer signifies the power of rationality but rather "an aesthetic state" of political imaging. While deconstructing the dialectic essence of ground for an exclusive imaging of power and history which cancels metaphysics' debt to morality, Nietzsche's aesthetic *Kehre* retains a problematic metaphysical disposition, particularly a tendency to make demands on appearances. Although his work in general tends to free imagination from the dominance of teleologic rationality, it incorporates a sense of that very dominance into the "faculty" of imagination. So, in the end, Nietzsche succeeds in espousing an *aesthetic* imperative. Let us briefly focus on this question.

For Nietzsche, the dialectic of subject and object is now seen within the horizon of "an aesthetic condition" of power. World and man are interwoven in the very "phenomenon" (*phainesthai*) of the work of art. This "phenomenon," however, is still viewed from the epistemic perspective of appearances which pervades the Kantian-Schopenhauerian philosophy. Even though ground has fallen from the power of noumenal rationality in Nietzsche's genealogy, presence (of ground) is nonetheless affirmed in the terrain of imagination's play of the wills to power.

Nietzsche's "new conception of world"[15] is that of the will to power of imagination (*Einbildungskraft*). An antinomy thus haunts his imaging of the political: imagination is not free of the will to power. The reader will have noted that Nietzsche's principle of ground, *der Wille zur Macht*, determines the spacings of imagination. Although it is clear that Nietzsche's genealogy seeks to free imagination from the dominance of the dialectic, it is just as clear that imagination is still in the service of the wills to power. Indeed, the intrametaphysical constellation of the political and the aesthetic serves to show the epistemic dependence of imagination upon the principle of the wills to power. Consequently, thinking as imaging, i.e., as "filming," is conceived of as mirroring the appearance-structure of modern subjectivity. This in turn means that the will, which is decentered from reason to imagination, takes on a new prominence in determining appearances within a domain of "filming" still muted by aesthetic presumptions of power. In effect, imagination as *Einbildungskraft* emerges as *Einbildungs-wille der Macht*. This priority of will in Nietzsche's transformation of the principle of ground maintains a mode of imaging whose thinking is in the service of a willing. Indeed, imaging is primarily willing for Nietzsche.[16] And imagination's own power is curtailed by the wills to power, by a language of presence which dominates the terrain of imagination. Imagination's enclosure in an aesthetic play of forces does not call into question the value of the wills to power, that is, Nietzsche's phenomenalism, which some prefer to call postmodernism. His radical questioning of metaphysics does not seem to demand an "aletheic" dismantling of the wills to power. It seems that power is a necessary condition for Nietzsche's own spacing at the limit of metaphysics.[17] While a disseminative laughter, signifying strength and courage, marks an epistemic undoing of metaphysics in his text, it mimes a political tradition reinscribed by imagination in the aesthetic economy of the wills to power.

Hovering between phantasy (*Einbildung*) and power (*Kraft*), the Nietzschean image of ground emerges as "the phantom in the center," from which his genealogy fascinates as it skids on the surface of an ontological order of rank. A new schema for imagination's play of genealogy becomes possible. It serves to unite phantasy and power in an aesthetic discourse attentive only to a distinctive imaginal sighting of ground. Within the unique spacing of phantasy and power, images of the wills to power break free of imagination's exclusive Apollinian demands of individuality. An anticipatory imaging reveals Nietzsche's genealogical deepening of aesthetic phenomenalism, a subversive counter-extension of the Kantian *episteme*. Neither cause nor ground determines Nietzsche's aesthetic interpretation of judgment unless ground is seen as archetype (*Urbild*) of imagination. The connection of representations that concern world and man is not pre-decided by an a priori category but by imagination's plurality of the wills to power.

It follows that will to power surges as image of power (*Kraft*) for the *will* in imagination. Nietzsche's emphasis on the concept of "a new power" does not surpass the limitations of imagination that his genealogy projects as imagination-in-the-will. A genealogical mode of judging is here grasped as an imaginal willing, indeed, as a "filming" that "wills" a certain dehiscence for imagination within the aesthetic plurality of the wills to power. Neither the will nor imagination, however, are free of power in Nietzsche's philosophy: "In every act of the will there is a ruling thought . . . The will is not only a complex of sensations and thinking, but it is above all an *affect*, and specifically the affect of the command."[18] Exceeding Nietzsche's texts, philosophy takes up the question of imagination's freedom from the wills to power. This "final spacing of metaphysics" awakens the principle of ground to a new text, one that announces imagination's withdrawal from its debt to an aesthetic economy of power.

IRONY OF POLITICAL IMAGING

The privilege of ground is by no means undone in Nietzsche's philosophy. On the contrary, this privilege is solidified by his monumental theory of power and history. Perhaps a particular metaphysical sense of ground such as the dialectic-noumenal dimension is weakened in his philosophy in general. Still, the aesthetic *Kehre* or turn from the tragic constellation of an Apollinian-Dionysian ground to an exclusive image of individuation or "great politics" remodels the principle of ground. Thus, in the later phase of Nietzsche's philosophy, ground is understood historically *and* super-historically. It emerges as the eternal play of forces, that "dark, driving, insatiably self-desiring power."[19] Which amounts to saying that history and power become conjoined, eternal super-historical forces in Nietzsche's monumental theory of ground. His view of power and history according to aesthetic-cultural criteria brings the socio-political reality closer to fiction. At times, it becomes impossible to distinguish between Nietzsche's serious remarks about the monumental past and future and his seemingly ironic, mythopoetic references to "great politics." In general, however, one can say that Nietzsche's play of deconstructing and constructing the essence of ground occasions an indelible conflict. This conflict lies between the "first" and "second" natures of his thought: the "first" being the disruptive, critical genealogy of reason with an Apollinian desire to seek infinite "imaginal" positions of interpretation; the "second" being determined by a pervasive Dionysian faith in humanity which is expressed in the demand for a *monumental* history, a theory of the will to power that is eternal. The first nature of thought implants a new instinct and habit into philosophical reflection by attempting to free reason from "reason" (or ground) for imagination. In striving to understand this Apollinian withdrawal, the second nature of thought misunderstands the Dionysian principle by cultivating an exclusive image of ground and subsuming imagination under the aegis of a historical magnanimity called will to power. Precisely this demand for what is great, for an unlimiting power, occasions as Nietzsche himself admits "the most terrible conflict."[20] A Hegelian after all, Nietzsche holds a monumental conception of power that serves an unhistorical truth whose ground is simply essence or "life alone, that dark, driving, insatiably self-desiring power." No astonishment at Nietzsche's radical hermeneutics, at his deconstructive instances of new meaning, should make us forget that the will to power concept, in spite of its interpretive amplitude, its defraction of epistemology, becomes a master-word with the eventual cultural irony of a "higher politics." Hence, Nietzsche's philosophical eccentricity turns out to be a brilliant, momentary suspension of metaphysics in the hopeful, monumental "filming" of a seemingly antifoundationalist political *Ereignis*.

Turning from a dialectical self-understanding of reason, Nietzsche's mode of "filming" stages an Apollinian play of illusion in which the aesthetic engagement of imagination and judgment accommodates the language of the wills to power. Initially wedded to a radicality of thought that outstrips inherited frames of "filming," Nietzsche's *skepsis* turns against itself in experiments which may be variously described as *films* of power, deeply entangled in an unjustifiable expansion of the concept of will. Entrapped within the aesthetic paradigm of a genealogy of willing, the Nietzschean manner of "filming," while providing "a continuous sign-chain of ever new interpretations,"[21] fails to attain philosophy's release from the taint of alternatives within the metaphysical enterprise.

2

◆

Postmodernism's Short Letter, Philosophy's Long Farewell

Modernity and the Illusion of Presence

An assessment of certain implications of modernity is necessary in order to understand the postmodern accounts of reflexivity beyond Nietzsche's genealogy. Modernity may be viewed as a hermeneutic of subjectivity beginning with Descartes' *Discourse on Method* and ending, perhaps, with Nietzsche's theory of the will to power. Between these two moments of philosophical genealogy, the texts of Kant, Hegel, and Marx, each in their own manner, underscore the marked difference between the commencement of modern thought and a thinking (*Denken*) that arguably signifies the end of modernity.

Descartes effectively announces thinking's radical withdrawal from a transcendent position of ground. While the principle of ground is no longer determined by a dialectic of nature, nature is subsumed under a new principle of ground, a dialectic of self-consciousness forming the methodological intentions of the subject's relation to world, in particular the mathematical ideal of knowledge. Reason is just beginning to be freed from the ontotheologic constraints of metaphysics. Descartes' radical subjectivity points to a dialectical elevation of interiority whose scientific purity of *mimesis* is then energized by Kant's dialectical mediations of practical reason. A transition from the pure presence of the ontological subject in Descartes to a practical presence of will and law in Kant introduces the socio-political operations of modernity. A leap from transcendental self-consciousness

21

to the power of self-determination opens authentic possibilities for a modernist constellation of theory and practice, which culminates in the spirit of the American Revolution. As the principle of ground is transformed to a *principium individuationis*, the voice of modernity bespeaks the "free individual," later to be actualized by the French Revolution. Thus modernity entails a plurality of discourses none of which is conceived independently of the other. As it crystallizes the interests of the subject from the viewpoint of a principle of ground that is essentially political in power, modernity gathers together the historical moments of subjectivity. More precisely, modernity signifies an ontology of the presence of power, that is, a radical transformation of the transcendental principle of ground to the political presence of the subject. Any attempt at soliciting the foundations of modernity is in turn bound to fail so long as the transition from a Cartesian formulation of ground, namely, subjectivity, is merely ontologized by means of cultural, that is, "political" power. Even Nietzsche's radical critique of philosophy remains modernist because of his attempts to legitimate the displacement of the principle of ground within an aesthetic ontology of the will to power.

What initially determines modernity as a highly mimetic form of dialectical thought is the Cartesian transition from a transcendent position of absolute ground to a transcendental presence of cognitive certainty. With Kant's critical philosophy, that certainty is relegated to an empirical understanding of reality while the principle of ground emerges as the dialectical difference of phenomenon and thing-in-itself. Here, the concept of ground itself becomes problematic for the first time in the history of philosophy. The *Critique of Pure Reason*, displacing the modernist foundation, announces a more radical phase of modernity. From now on modernity is conceived not only as epistemological transformation of ground but, more importantly, as a mode of thought which discerns the very principle of ground to be a dialectic of illusion. By the same token, Nietzsche begins to view the concept of ground as an illusion of presence which envelops political and sociocultural intentions of modernity. This paradoxical extension of modernity is exemplified by Marx's ideological critique of consciousness and his negation of a particular socioeconomic presence. And yet, Marx's dialectical humanism is only one phase of the paradox of modernity. A more passionate self-criticism of modernity springs from Schopenhauer and Wagner, whose understanding of ground as aesthetic willing evokes the question whether the enhanced transformation of the idea of ground to the sphere of social reality, as discerned in Marx's texts, is not as illusory as the classical identity of reason and ground or the Cartesian attempt to dethrone the absolute by means of subjectivity. But then again, Wagner's deconstruction of history takes place under the aegis of "nature," which tends to reinforce the principle of ground from a metaphysically immanent perspective similar to that of Feuerbach and Nietzsche, so that modernity is still measured by the illusion of presence.[1]

From this brief glance at some of the metamorphoses of the principle of ground, we see that modernity is a dynamic dialectic embedded in *geistige Leiblichkeit*.[2] This enlivening physiology thrives on restlessness and tensions disclosed in the political and social forms of metaphysical rupture. So regarded, modernity extends the principle of ground to a mode of thinking replete with revolutionary, introspectionist intentions linked to a truth presencing itself in a sociocultural space. Even in deconstructing ground, modernity, always conscious of its desire for ground, does not make it possible to sever the concept of ground from the dialectic nature of its principle, until imagination withdraws from the classical power of reason and the certainty of its subjective essence. Thus, while resisting the idea that ground is the social essence of freedom, modernity, in spite of its power of self-criticism, is inextricably bound to that idealized notion. And even at its limit, in the very attempt to undercut the metaphysical dimensions of closure, modernity is not free of the illusions of presence.[3]

IMAGINATION'S TURN TO FILMING

Obversely, Heidegger's thinking marks the beginning of an "ontological" exit from the logocentric modernity of western culture. This beginning evokes a speculative, postmodern mood which emphasizes that a radical trembling can only come from the *outside* (*M*, 134). Postmodern thought, however, does not render the *outside* as the dialectic *other* of the inside, for its projective reading breaks with the terrain of Hegel's idealist dialectic. This section will seek to convey a sense of the variety of postmodern thought in relation to a philosophic and cultural crisis of imagination.

The western edifice of egocentrism is eroded when the *outside* is no longer viewed as an infrastructural or superstructural model, that is, as an economic, political, or cultural phenomenon subject to the reflexibility of a patriarchal impulse. Postmodern thought sketches the *outside* as a discontinuous image (*Bild*) of contemporary culture, which modern subjectivity is unable to illuminate. By inscribing the *outside* into the traces of *Ereignis*, *gram*, or *différance*, a mode of thinking emerges which does not replicate the transcendental moorings of the dialectic.

Derrida's deconstructive operations, Foucault's genealogical discourse, Deleuze's schizo-analysis and nomad thought, and Lyotard's concept of the postmodern condition (to mention a few postmodern strategies) develop a "plural style" of thinking which frees imagination from the anthropocentric legacy of metaphysics. Dislodging imagination from the spatial and temporal constraints of understanding, thinking radically questions the theoretical and practical efficacy of a philosophy ensnared by the power of a transcendental ego in its a priori, a posteriori, transcendental, political, and socio-economic manifestations. The "subject," who seems securely fastened to the conceptual "sitting-flesh" of the humanistic ideals of "excessive self-entanglement,"[4] is no more able to restore the voice of Descartes' *ego cogitans* to its pristine epistemic vitality than she is willing to dwell poetically in the *city* of language, whose metaphor of production glimmers doubtfully in the light of a fading self.

The displacement of subjectivity does not destroy the *inside* of being, not even the discursive representations of self-consciousness. Instead, deconstruction has all the characteristics of a *relève* (*eine Aufhebung*) of the *inside*, which is at the point of greatest proximity to a *Lichtung* of the *outside*. What decentering rejects is precisely the dominance of oppositional philosophizing and dialectical ideologizing. It disrupts the continual logocentric spurning of subject against object, a spurning that purports to free subject from object but merely retains subject as object.

Deconstruction's intellectual audacity, therefore, grants thinking a dialogical encounter between *inside* and *outside* in which a postmodern dispersion of the subject does not correspond to the transcendental self-relations of *Truth and Method*. On the contrary, deconstruction announces a "change of terrain," notably a place where language lets thinking be, and where thinking in turn understands language in its openness (*M*, 135). By pointing to a self that lies between *inside* and *outside*, language claims a "different self," one that is not identical with the historically regional inside of self-consciousness.

In the attempt to burst through the conceptual repressions of modern epistemology, the postmodern mood recognizes the Kantian dilemma of "what to do with imagination." In view of *das freie Spiel* ("free play") of subjective judgment, imagination appears to be free in the absence of the use of a concept. While a sense of freedom emerges in its aesthetic movement, imagination still dwells in the castle of subjectivity, glancing at the open field of judgment without participating in *das Freie des Offenen* ("what is free in the open"). Given this view, Kant's analysis of aesthetic taste deflects from the traditional method but falls short of questioning the legitimation of overseeing imagination from the egophanic perspectives of reflective judgment. The *Critique of Judgment* manifests imagination's turn from a regional, transcendental sphere of understanding to the aesthetic space of reflective judgment, but fails to achieve the freedom of imagination initially conceived to be possible in imagination's own play of presence and absence. Instead, imagination extends itself to a supersensible, transcendental sphere in which a new limitation is determined for itself. This new limitation belongs to Kant's moral predilection and ineluctably supersedes the aesthetic project of freeing imagination from epistemic egocentrism. Kant's formal dialectic animated by moral impulse transforms imagination's "free play" into teleologic acts of judgment.

Every aspect of the postmodern mood reveals the discontent that arises from the difficulty of overcoming Kant's intertranscendental, *moral* displacements of imagination in the *Critique of Judgment*. Hence, postmodernism emerges as a restless resident in the metaphysical house of modernity. As a new guest, weary of looking at the same old objects, postmodernism writes a short letter of gratitude to philosophy in view of "the necessity of a certain point of departure," markedly, that of subjectivity. In its technological twilight, subjectivity is not, as Habermas suggests, dead like modernism, but is, instead, admitted by postmodernism to the subversive destiny of thinking language as *différance*. *Ecriture*, as thinking, is a new writing that weaves and interlaces the continuous and discontinuous motifs of philosophy's farewell. The radical trembling that can only come from the *outside* is now inscribed on the concealed terrain of another *inside*, "where" a nonconceptual reflection of the subject reveals a self-consciousness which is itself overshadowed by thinking's playful itinerary of imaginal sighting.[5]

As Heidegger's *Lichtung* makes possible Derrida's deconstructive critique of binary thinking, so *écriture* grants an awareness of a late postmodern dissipation of the self as filming.[6] From the perspectives of filming, the self is initially revealed as a process of "images" gathering and exceeding the "structural" imaginal formations of *inside* and *outside*, the political, social, economic, and cultural modifications of production, without manipulating these modifications ontotheologically.[7] The postmodern condition of filming, therefore, points to human apperception as imagination infinitely at work in the discontinuous process of relating judgment to countermetaphysical discursive practices.

The technological destiny of being, which reflects contemporary western culture, is challenged by imagination's freedom from the *mythos* of philosophy's idiom, the "white mythology" of Reason. The task of thinking, then, is to measure this new freedom and to avoid the possible hazards of imagination's "free play" with time. Thinking must confront the egocentric continuity revealed in certain modes of technological developments, in particular, the effects of the military imagination. The power structures of late capitalism and diverse socialism may exploit the creative freedom of imagination by subjecting the play of signifiers to the futural signified of nuclear dissemination. These immoderate political games of imagination may result in negative possibilities even in imagination's release from the transcendental signified. However, these military escapades should not prevent us from affirming imagination in a Dionysian sense, nor should they lead us to disregard the vigil of thinking in relation to the nuclear shadow of the metaphysical network.

I turn now more concretely to a postmodern transgression of the thinking self. How can imagination be diverted from the transcendental direction of a subjective *Verstand/Vernunft* interplay? I have already alluded to the invagination of *ego cogitans* into imaginal formations of imagination and into a play of being that gathers, inevitably, in a constellation of word, music, and profuse images of temporality. Here, filming may appropriately characterize the diffuse movements of the self within the artistic postmodern epoch of imagination.

Filming, in our strategic naming, does not primarily belong to the technico-functional structures of cinematography, nor to the more conspicuous ontic practices of producing, acting, editing, and directing. A postontological reading suggests that filming is related to imaginal ecstasies of time. I will briefly delineate traces of the subject fading into imaginal formations of past, present, and future in the luminous process of filming. These reflections are merely preliminary.

Postmodern thought rejects philosophy's protracted contempt for the priority of images over *Begriff* ("concept"). It fails to acclaim a self whose being is readily present and defined in modern theories of society, religion, and science; instead, it exposes a self that is not subject to an epistemic dominance of master narratives (*grand recit*). Filming, which is not restricted to instrumental, ideological, profitable functions or any other ontic interests, inscribes the self and its imaginal formations into an *aletheia* of imagination, while still affirming a Dionysian breakdown of the relationship between signifiers. Filming shows a signifier that has lost its signified and has thereby been transformed into an imaginal "being." The self *had been* such a signifier; now, the self *is* an imaginal constellation. Thus, the scene of the self has moved away from it-self. Ob-scenity emerges.[8]

Filming radically displaces metaphysical representations. Its ob-scenity reveals a *glissement* of self in imagination's "free play" of judgment. In this terrain, the self appears as a being-in-imagination. As a rapidly fading concept, the self "exists" as a collage of images not linked to the progression from past to present into future, nor simply to a circle of temporality, unless this circle reveals an eclipse of the self alongside the inside/outside imaginal formations of difference. The self is shown neither as appearance nor as noumenon in the perceptions, actions, and emotions of imaginal formations. In the postmodern flow of an imaginal subject, there is no showing of a theoretical or a practical will, of a fetish or a commodity.

Still, a self may be uncovered: in filming, *Dasein* may be viewed as enabling viewer, director, producer, writer, actor, and critic to see, make, write, and reflect upon a montage of images. More than a *self*, however, it is *filming* that exists. To amplify Godard's Cartesian mime: "Je pense, donc le cinema existe."[9] The postmodern impulse to participate in imagination's play of philosophy's farewell reveals a unique mode of filming which conceptual directors of metaphysics have only vaguely considered, even in the most critical moments of high modernity. A "filmic" dissemination of the self may provide fruitful metonymic notes of reflection on contemporary culture. Such notes may suggest that filming illuminates a radical displacement of *Dasein*.

In formulating the process of filming, it is important not to epistemologize the "releasing of imagination's own intrinsic [traditional] reflexivity."[10] As Derrida writes: "The continuous process of making [a subject matter; in this case, the *matter* of the *subject*] explicit, moving toward an opening, risks sinking into the autism of closure" (*M*, 135). The transgression from *ego cogitans* to filming is not to be interpreted as a "false exit" from philosophy; rather, it is a question of "anonymous necessity" (*M*, 134). The effects of a radical trembling, therefore, do not lie in a hermeneutic relation of filming and *Lichtung*. Nor should one impute to filming an epistemology or social theory with renewed metaphysical interests. Unlike the dominance of representational thinking, filming provides a distinctive way of encountering *Dasein*, whose traces of past and future are no longer present to representation, yet are "present" to the imaginal formations of the postmodern scene. Filming, then, allows a fleeting self to emerge in the very disruption of imaginal identity and difference. Lyotard partially alludes to this process when he writes: "A self does not amount to much, but no self is an island; each exists in a fabric of relations that is now more complex and mobile than ever before."[11] Heidegger hints at the identity-difference problem of the self by relating the question of imagination to a nondialectical mode of imaginal sighting.[12] A narrative reading of the vanishing self is also invited by Derrida's openness of *écriture*, which can be further developed in regard to a "filmic" occlusion of imagination. Such an occlusion replaces "Kant's turn toward [aesthetic] subjectivity with a [postmodern] turn toward the play of images."[13] Hence, a "filmic" self is unveiled as attending to past and future images among fleeting moments of presence, while paradoxically yielding to fading images of past and future in the absence of radical self-presence. Accordingly, the texture of relations between the outside/inside imaginal formations of the self is, indeed, what Sallis calls "a play of occlusion," if by occlusion we understand "the absorption of the intelligible to the sensible and the collapse of metaphysical distinctions."[14]

In dismantling subjectivity, postmodernism exceeds the subject-object polarity and projects a filming of self which displaces the logocentric images of understanding in the course of imagination's play of absence and presence. In this chapter, we have only begun to think the *outside* from the in-finite imaginal formations of imagination's "free play," "thereby inhabiting more naively and more strictly than ever the *inside* one declares one has deserted" (*M*, 135).

The irony of filming's *eros* does not lead to a new determination of the intelligible. On the contrary, the possibilities of filming reveal that "images in their play are also turned toward something which they image, and in turning toward images, one inevitably passes through them in such fashion as in the end to be turned away from them."[15] John Sallis briefly alludes to the obstruction of postmodernism in general and to *filming* in particular when he writes:

> The metaphysical distinction between intelligible and sensible is radically displaced, decisively unsettled, by the turn to the play of imaging, for in that play there is incessant opening and closing of the distance between the tradition, between its beginning in the Platonic dialogues, and what has been thematized as intelligible and sensible. The play of imaging is nothing but the play of occlusion itself.[16]

Nothing seems to escape this play—a play that must still be articulated within the spacings of thinking and filming. Within these spacings, one may question the postmodern dissolution of subject, primarily because postmodernism shows that "we are both too much within and too much without metaphysics."[17]

POSTMODERNISM AND 'PHAINESTHAI'

Yet, undoubtedly, postmodernism radically questions the legitimacy of the principle of ground. Certain postmodern modalities must therefore be considered with regard to the ambiguity of postmodernism's relation to metaphysics and to the disruptive operations of filming.

Let us begin with reason's withdrawal from ground. Nietzsche's aesthetic turn to the Apollinian play of images, which intensifies Kant's displacement of imagination in the *Critique of Judgment*, sets the stage for a radical questioning of ground. Heidegger pursues the urgency of this task in an essay entitled *Vom Wesen des Grundes*. Here he invites thinking to a postmodern questioning of the privilege granted to the principle of sufficient reason, the perennial mark of metaphysics. The question of ground, which is accorded to the essence of truth, is thought to be a problem of transcendence. But transcendence is not a transcendent position. It is the open terrain in which the imaginal play of judgment exceeds the principle of ground. For Heidegger, *Transzendenz* signifies a "moving event," such that *Dasein*'s falling into world is no longer bound up with the perspective of nature but with imagination's distinctive work of art. The transgression from reason as ground to imagination as disclosure of world reveals world in its mimetic displacement. Reason is now aligned to a world that is neither an object of praxis nor an idea of the thinking subject. Instead, world emerges as *Spiel* ("play") of imagination's power, signifying a postmodern advance into a "capital terrain" (*ausgezeichneten Bezirk*) of freedom.[18] Heidegger does not claim that freedom approximates ground but, paradoxically, that freedom is the origin of ground. To be free is to be free *for* ground, not dependent upon it.

The break with modernism, then, begins with an imaginal deconstruction of ground in which essence is removed from the very idea of ground. When this happens, essence is dislodged from its classical embeddedness in nature and is regarded as *Un-wesen* in relation to the abyss (*Ab-grund*).[19] A distinctive interlacing of *Un-wesen*, *Ab-grund*, and *Welt* subverts the domain of subjectivity and its principle of ground. Imagination emerges as a dehiscent play of the abyss (*Das Aufbrechen des Abgrundes*).[20] Here a mimetic waning points already to a site (*Ort*) of filming in which world as image is neither copy, symbol, nor place of repose. As temporal shining of imagination's "play-ground," filming breaks out of enframing, the logocentric "filming" of essence, and may now be viewed as belonging to what Heidegger calls "the event of image" (*das Geschehnis des Bildes*, *ED*, 121). "Image, therefore, images the site of the unconcealing concealment (of *aletheia*)."[21] The truth of filming lies in imagination's play of mimetic degrounding. Thus, Heidegger grants thinking the preeminence of *phainesthai* as "free play" of shining without shining *for* someone or *at* something. Indeed, he opens up a terrain of thought that previously had not been possible in light of the precarious metaphysical identity of reason and ground. The very naming of *phainesthai* frees being from the ground of self-consciousness, and thereby discontinues a tradition of representational thinking for which "shining" is merely a mode of dialectic. Heidegger's *phainesthai* denotes a decisive turning point in the history of philosophy, one in which the *Spielraum* ("play-ground") of being is thematized from the perspectives of the power of imagination rather than of the dominance of the principle of sufficient reason. While the texts of Kant and Nietzsche may be read to permit this shift, Heidegger's phenomenology makes the filmic formations of postmodernism explicit together with the risks of a radical opening of reason.

MIMETIC DE-GROUNDING

Postmodernism, then, can be traced to a Heideggerian breakthrough of *phainesthai*, in particular, to the phenomenological de-limitation of the principle of ground. Let us focus more on this subversion of ground, which occurs in a singular turn to *phainesthai*, a unique shining, which for filming appears neither in appearances nor in the things themselves. *Phainesthai* provides a relation peculiar to lighting that reveals world as image. Exceeding the vertical structure of *mimesis*, this "relation" is neither subject nor object of filming. Filming excludes the very question of a showing of object for subject. Instead, its shining occurs as imaginal event beyond the closed, dialectic relation of theory and practice.[22]

A Heideggerian perspective on filming is revealed (*bewegt sich*) in discourse. "Wir sind ein Sprachgeschehnis." Indeed, discourse belongs to *phainesthai*.[23] What is sighted in discourse is the event of image, world coming into presence in its withdrawal from ground. Discourse then becomes ever more difficult in the course of technology's power of enframing or *Dasein*'s falling into the abyss of *mimesis*, into *Un-wesen*, the "essence" that is taken from freedom. And yet, discourse always venture into a "higher doing," into the event of image, into a shining we are least prepared for, a *phainesthai* unheard of in metaphysics. What is made manifest in Heidegger's text is a *phainesthai* that carries *Dasein* across the mimetic abyss. *Phainesthai* serves as a passageway from the enframing power of the political will toward a filmic terrain of freedom. Consequently, Heidegger interrupts modernity with a discursive determination of *phainesthai* that consists in understanding freedom as *diagoge*, a passing through, a going across the mimetic abyss of "history," world straying from ground, in some manner, even opening itself to the ground of going astray (*die Irre*). Heidegger writes: "Man does not merely stray into errancy. He is always astray in errancy" (*BW*, 135). What is sighted, therefore, in man's falling into world, is the continual filming, the strife without which thinking falls from its matter. In his lecture *Vom Wesen der Wahrheit*, Heidegger examines the issue of the delimitation of ground from the perspective of filmic errancy, "which belongs to the inner constitution of *Dasein* into which historical man is admitted" (*BW*, 136). The image shines forth as an inimitable event—discourse passing through, hoping to defer the oppression of nihilism, the image of *Dasein* falling into filming. But surely, *phainesthai* and filming are not one and the same.[24]

What I have called filming is a postmodern extension of *phainesthai*. In its subversive de-lighting of images, filming is related to but not dependent upon *phainesthai*.[25] The form of this relation lies in Heidegger's disruption of ground. But beyond this form how are filming and *phainesthai* related? *Phainesthai* is a propaedeutic shining which comes to presence in the event of image, granting imagination a playful terrain which exposes the mimetic absence of the subject. With regard to filming, we are challenged by a more radical turn within the mimetic play of imagination: *mimesis*' turn to an imaging without image, to a distinctive play of withdrawal from being. Thus, filming proper deconstructs the principle of ground much more radically than Heidegger's thinking, for *phainesthai* is ultimately still ontological. By virtue of its relation to being, *phainesthai* does not denude *mimesis* entirely. Filming's relation to *mimesis*, on the other hand, is quite different since it does not have the ontological form imputed to *phainesthai* by Heidegger. Filming is not contingent upon a hermeneutic sight of presence that still guides the "photo-ontocentric" naming of *phainesthai*.

Only on condition of *Dasein*'s falling into filming does the text of postmodernism speak such that in its sundry reactions to high modernism, dissension (*Entzweiung*) shines forth. This dissension does not denote a "list of postmodernisms" characterizing various literary and architectural styles. It leads, instead, to a view of postmodernism as "the power that sets in motion" (*die treibende Kraft*), the rupture (*Zerissenheit*) of modernity (*Se*, 291). This de-grounding and delimiting of *mimesis* makes it possible to think of errancy as the "open site" of filming. All the themes related to filming no longer constitute the vertical structure of *mimesis* with its illusion of presence. What is sighted in *Dasein*'s falling into filming is the image of world as power of errancy. Here Heidegger thinks of filming as a discursive image (*bildende Rede*), that is, as discourse of reason falling from ground toward dissension. Philosophical thinking is now "torn apart" (*zerissen*), as reason's mimetic debt to ground fades into *phainesthai*. Torn between the illusion of ground which modernity bespeaks and the abyss of freedom which postmodernism grants, thinking sees the irony of dissension, the radical rupture of identity—the filmic strife of thinking and being. It is absurd to think that we can return to modernity or its remote origins. Thinking does not aspire to undertake such a romantic venture. Its task is to understand the erosion of ground in terms of world as "image of errancy," without negating reason's wakening from the metaphysical sleep of presence. High modernity's collision with postmodernism sets in motion a dissension that enables discourse to see errancy not as a political image of ground but as the imaginal disruption of the conditions for such a possibility.

HEIDEGGER IN THE EPOCH OF FILMING

In the wake of the fractured scene of metaphysics, is filming philosophy's new thesis? A radical trembling? The "hole" in the "whole" of the dialectic? If we assume that filming is the beginning of an *Abbruch* from philosophy, a de-lighting of reason's *phaos*, what can be said about the "movement" of its force (*vis*) and seeing (*visum*)? From this point of view, what does filming signify? Perhaps, we should first discuss, rather briefly, what filming does not signify. Filming, as it is named here, is not disclosed in Leonardo da Vinci's notion of *camera obscura*, nor in Thomas Edison's invention of the first workable motion picture camera. Indeed, filming does not belong in the archives of cinema and detailed studies of filmmaking. A historical and cultural theory concerning the very possibility of filming would certainly include such studies and many other cinematographic considerations. But our focus in this investigation is to expose filming as a non-photologocentric mode of judgment which accounts for a postmodern interplay of *Denken* and *Einbildungskraft*.

In modern metaphysics, we encounter the beginning of this mode of thinking in Kant's *Critique of Judgment*, in Nietzsche's *Birth of Tragedy*, and, more recently, in Heidegger's writings of the 1920s and 30s. From a genealogical perspective, we may also discover filming in the epistemic, ontologic, and aesthetic issues of a metaphysics of subjectivity. The hidden history of filming, however, goes back much further and may initially have been presented, somewhat negatively, in the configurations of Plato's discourses on *Eros* in the *Symposium*. We can see that the question of filming is one that has not been raised explicitly with regard to a metaphysical text. In short, the history of philosophy, at least from Plato to Spinoza, has consistently repressed the notion of imaging and confined its importance to a logocentric view of reason. Even in the early part of the nineteenth century, after the invention of the camera, a renowned philosopher complains that his era "prefers the image to the thing, the copy to the original representation of reality, appearance to being."[26] No doubt, Ludwig Feuerbach did not appreciate Kant's attempt to loosen the subject's dialectic dependency on rationality in order to free imagination for an aesthetic deconstruction (*Bahnung*) of subjectivity.

In retracing the philosophies of Kant, Nietzsche, Heidegger, and Derrida, in which the name of filming does not yet arise, an economy of filming, however, has already come into view. It begins with Kant's idea of the schema as pure synthesis that makes images possible. In our proposal to address filming as thinking (as *denkendes Wort*), we are inscribing a "mimetic" elevation of schematism from the transcendental realm of understanding into an opening (*das Freie des Offenen*) of reason. Although Kant limits the schematic activity of imagination to the empirical direction of understanding, he still claims that schematism is "an art concealed in the depths of the human soul, whose real modes of activity nature is hardly likely ever to allow us to discover and to have open to our gaze" (*CR*, 183). The significance of this "concealed art" (*verborgene Kunst*) is examined in the *Critique of Judgment*, in which the attempt is made to dislodge imagination from the praxeological space of the epistemic interests of *Verstand*. This effort serves to efface the theoretical confinement of imagination to the schematism of understanding without withdrawing from the schematic activity of imaging per se. Traces of filming are foregrounded in the aesthetic enterprise of Kant's critical philosophy: a schematic dehiscence that "scatters" (Gr. *speiro*; Lat. *spargere*) the schemas from the domain of understanding, disseminates images into the open of "imaginal judging," preparing the way for a Heideggerian disclosure of filming.

In this Kantian endeavor, the aesthetic idea gives "imagination occasion to spread itself over a host of related representations" beyond the impasse of spatial and temporal intuitions. "So in the case of an aesthetic idea the *understanding* with its concepts never reaches the entire inner intuition that the imagination has" (*CJ*, 216). It appears then that imagination in its free schematic presentation invariably exceeds representational essentiality by inducing "such a wealth of thought as would never admit comprehension in a definite concept" (*CJ*, 217). Accordingly, imaginal judging in its aesthetic significance dismantles the analytic principle of reflection. In an equivocally postmodern sense, Kant grants imagination "a free play" of thought that is no longer determined by an objective principle of ground. The shift from an epistemic to an aesthetic spacing allows imagination the freedom to reflect upon a different grounding, one that lets *Anschauung* be. Insofar as *Anschauung* and *Ur-teil* mirror each other in a distinctive mimetic mode of conceiving works of art, a possibility of filming, albeit limited, arises.

The capacity of thought in imagination, which eventually leads us to posit filming, emerges in its aesthetic power of judgment. As imagination strives to expand its imaginal judging, it sinks back into itself, challenged by what it desires the most: the open, the infinite spacings of reason. Kant underscores the importance of the mimetic connection between imagination and reason. Indeed, without reason an imaginal play of judging is purely arbitrary. Nonetheless, filming, as will be shown in this text, is not the product of an aesthetic constellation of reason and imagination. On the contrary, it involves a radical displacement of and an epistemic disjunction between reason and imagination, so that neither imagination nor reason can be properly targeted by judgment. It follows then, that judgment seeks its freedom from a dissonant interplay of imagination and reason in order to discern the fissures of a sublime *mimesis*.

In his description of the sublime, Kant seeks to formulate a "discontinuous" relation between reason and imagination. The sublime, lacking definite form, yet emerging as a "reflective disposition" (*Gemüt*), surpasses the boundaries of imagination. How will imagination relate to this radical aesthetic concern for the sublime? Kant's aesthetic turn from nature to the power of subjective reflection refers imagination to reason. This suggests that imagination is invited by reason to engage in a reflective operation of apprehending but not comprehending pure synthesis. Thinking, therefore, reserves its imaginal place for "the matter itself," what Kant also calls the unconditional or the invisible. While the invisible is the nonobjective condition for the possibility of the sublime, it tears itself from the power of imagination in order to show reason that imagination's aesthetic mirroring of itself precludes the ethical terrain of the will. Even so, imagination cannot remain its own free play of *mimesis*. Without yielding to a de-mimesis of filming, imagination cannot film its way out of the teleological order of reason. Ultimately, Kant's radical aesthetic turn toward a moral ground is a metaphysical boomerang which returns imagination to the principle of sufficient reason. Whence imagination's "purpose requires that reason has an idea that moves sufficiently for reflective judgment" (*CJ*, 346). But an attentive reader will note that this is not the last word in the *Critique of Judgment*. Indeed, Kant admits that he cannot claim that a moral principle of ground is certain for an imaginal use of reason. "Hence it is merely for the practical use of our reason that we have established sufficiently the actuality of a supreme author who legislates morality" (*CJ*, 346).

This continual tension in Kant's text elicits a change of terrain for imagination: a sublime beginning for filming reveals a displacement of the principle of ground, but not without "the character of the power of reason as such" (*CJ*, 346). Imagination is thoroughly governed by a *movement* (*Bewegung*) in reason which limits judgment to the pursuit of the infinite. Judgment, therefore, enjoins on reason and imagination a constellation which refers to aesthetic itineraries of thought. But this filmic motif is caught in the unlimitedness (*Unbegrenztheit*) of the sublime, ever promoting the finality of Kant's probing moral presencing. Only nature in its chaotic power violates the principle of finality. An aesthetic orientation of reason rests upon an understanding of the sublime as absence of ground, as abyss, the uncanny guest of nihilism in the Kantian edifice of metaphysics. The transgression of finality which Kant attributes to nature, postmodern thought ascribes to the power of imagination and, indirectly, to filming. Still, the sublime may be regarded as unboundedness, not within the horizon of teleology but within an imaginal power of reason whose thinking attunes judgment to be undesignedly free. In transgressing Kant's critique of judgment, imagination collides with the sublime, as judgment is no longer aligned with finality. Withdrawing from finality, the sublime is radically transformed, infinitely nonpurposive.[27] In effect, the sublime emerges as the beauty of judgment's gap, an aesthetic bewilderment de-lighting in the formlessness of its new "reference point." As judgment is released from the teleologic power of reason and the transcendental interests of imagination, it sees itself at the edge of a filmic precipice touching the limits of imagination's new site. Here, imagination is free for the power of its own nature, its "chaos . . . its wildest and most rueless disarray and devastation" (*PS*, 246). Sublimity is still discerned in nature as imaginal dehiscence, invariably an opening for filming, the beginning of a "geneafilmic" mode of judging in which the matter of thinking is neither metaphysics nor science. Accordingly, filming relates "the end of philosophy" as discourse to technology's *to pragma auto* in its diffusion of imaginal formations.

The pertinent traits that assign a disclosive opening to filming are in a singular text entitled *Die Begründung des neuzeitlichen Weltbildes durch die Metaphysik*, which Heidegger initially delivered at the University of Freiburg.[28] In this lecture, Heidegger views the modern age from a horizon of truth that comes to pass in what he calls *imaginatio*. He writes: "The key event of modern times is the conquest of world as image" (*QT*, 134). The question of filming commences with this "imaginal" point of departure. In reading world as image, Heidegger claims that the modern age arises out of an illuminative interweaving of world and man in which, nevertheless, subjection, domination, and control—in short, representation—still play a significant role. Man appears as *subjectum imaginum*, and world as (re)production of images. At first glance, one wonders whether this reading of *Dasein* makes recourse to a Cartesian formulation of being, or, perhaps to a Nietzschean hermeneutic which is then transformed into an ontological analysis of modernity. For, in Heidegger's own words, "man becomes the representative of that which is," and "image means the formation (*Gebilde*), that is to say, the product of man's producing which represents and sets before" (*QT*, 134). This particular *Auslegung*, however, holds only for a determination of "imaging" in an ontic, technical, and intracultural unfolding which accords with "filming" as that which filming actually deconstructs in its imaginal judging. Thus, while Heidegger still underlines an understanding of world within representation, representation is disengaged from a metaphysical structure of the will by means of a filming which ironically turns away from "filming."

In a sublime opening, filming "extends itself out into a space withdrawn from representation" (*QT*, 136). Heidegger's thinking, therefore, is indicative of postmodernism without being postmodern. Indeed, thinking may indicate an interest in the question of the postmodern without succumbing to postmodernity. Here it is important to distinguish between the now fashionable constellation of thinking and postmodernism and the question concerning the matter of thinking. The latter may be philosophical without being postmodern; the former may be intellectually seductive without being relative to thought. The difference lies in filming, that is, in the relation between thinking's matter and thinking the "matter." Within the limits of this determination, filming is the matter of thinking, a radical shining, and a thinking of this shining. In one sense, therefore, filming parallels postmodern thought, yet in terms of a sublime opening it directs its gaze beyond postmodernity. Exceeding a hermeneutic of being, filming judges "filming," or dialectical reflection, and turns to a thinking which disrupts the principle of ground. Such an itinerary of thought affirms *écriture* so long as we understand writing as the possibility of *via rupta*, "the path that is broken, beaten, *fracta*," what Derrida calls "violent spacing."[29] In turn, filming may be expounded as a postmodern displacement of metaphysics in its effort to free imagination from the transcendental constraints of *Verstand* in favor of a more privileged play of *Vernunft*. This indicates an "imaginally" derived mode of judging which is not in any sense prerational, irrational, or philosophically irresponsible. On the contrary, at issue is a kind of *Besinnung* that has the courage to question the truth of its own presuppositions, including the diversity of its interests. So regarded, filming is not an imaging without reflection. In its genealogic discontinuity, it does not even involve imaging. Instead, filming announces an opening of judgment (*das ur-teilende Offene*), a de-lighting of being by exceeding a horizonal *mimesis*.

When Heidegger disentwines world from the transcendental concept of idea in the name of a turning to (*Einkehr*) images, he makes it possible to speak of filming as *Besinnung* of imagination. In attempting to resolve the cosmic antinomy of pure reason, Heidegger inscribes a filmic mode of *Verstehen* beyond the egophanic sphere of *Verstand* into a terrain of imagination not subject to representational discourse *more metaphysico*. The relation of imagination to representation must now be seen differently.

In filming as *Besinnung*, representations of man and world do not emerge according to empirical or transcendental paradigms but rather as images of an increasingly diffuse constellation of being which Heidegger calls *Einblitz*. His 1949 lecture, *Die Kehre*, grants a more determined place to imagination's self-opening than *Die Zeit des Weltbildes*. Indeed, one could argue that Heidegger introduces "imaginal modalities" which name what he calls "the constellation of being," the essence of technology, the coming-into-presence of *Gefahr*. These "modalities" are an initial index of what can be discerned in filming. Named *Einsicht*, *Einblick*, and *Einblitz*, literally, these terms mean a seeing, a glancing, a flashing respectively, each prefixed by *ein* to underscore the epoch of being as a constellation of imaginal sightings. Hence, images light up as beings-in-imagination. Within these dispersed "imaginal formations" of contemporary technology, filming denotes a reflective desire to disrupt the path of *logos*. With regard to being's filmic *Kehre*, we are reminded here of Nietzsche's remark that we may assume we are merely images in "the bright open-space of world" (*QT*, 47).

More specifically, filming, in Heidegger's sense of *Besinnung*, extricates images from the hermeneutic power of establishing a new presence, images trapped within enframing. Filming must be differentiated from filmmaking, the showing of films, including an intracultural disclosure of electronic imagery. It must also be differentiated from a quantitative proliferation of images, described "negatively" by Heidegger as revealing the modern age in its unlimited power-play of "calculating, planning, and molding [of] all things" (*QT*, 135). Since filming unfolds a postdialectic task of thinking, it must be accorded a discursive countermetaphysical reflection (*Besinnung*) in accordance with an imaginal play of judgment. Such a play need not be dominated by the dialectical comportment of contemporary technique sighted in *Ge-stell*. Nor should *Ge-stell*, in light of the "epoch of being," be viewed negatively. Enframing participates in the very turning of being. Most remarkably, enframing dawns as the rule of "filming," "the essential glance of being" (*der Wesensblick des Seins*) (*TK*, 46). In turn, a double play of occlusion prompts the very activity of thinking: that of enframing (*Ge-stell*) and that of the danger (*Gefahr*). This imaginal coalescence makes possible the theoretico-practical transformation of subjective and objective representations into a filmic dissemination of images in which being comes into presence as *Einblitz*, as a tectonic turn to lighting. For Heidegger such an ontological operation is only a pre-image (*Vorbild*) of filming, a constellation of enframing and danger occurring in being's own turn, which reveals the crisis of our epoch:

> The turn of the danger comes to pass suddenly. In this turn, the clearing of the essence of being suddenly lights up. This sudden self-lighting is the lightning-flash (*Blitzen*). It brings itself into its own brightness, which it itself both brings along and brings in. When in the turning of danger, the truth of being flashes, the essence of being lights itself up. Then the truth of the essence of being turns and enters in. (*QT*, 44)

Filming, without being named as such in this passage, reveals "the event of withdrawal"in a constellation of images related but not confined to enframing. Indeed, enframing illuminates the "event of withdrawal" in a "filming," falling, and veiling of being. "And yet—in all the disguising belonging to enframing, the truth of being flashes" (*QT*, 47), tracing a discontinuous interplay of thinking and imagination (*Einbildungskraft*), which, in its images of enframing and danger, prompts a paradoxical mode of filming.

While thinking as filming emerges as a veiling of the dialectic-hermeneutic circle, this veiling is still the "essential glance" of being. The danger of enframing lies not in falling from the authoritative technique of hermeneutics but in disallowing imagination to be free of all mimetic standards of measure. Consequently, what is truly dangerous is ontology's movement *without* the turn. Still, being grants itself a turn to *Ge-stell*, which detracts the subject from imposing its mimetic rule and commences the event of philosophy's withdrawal:

> What withdraws may even concern and claim man more essentially than anything present that strikes and touches him. The event of withdrawal could be what is most present in all our present, and so infinitely exceeds the actuality of everything actual.[30]

While the epoch of being in its diverse showings is not grounded dialectically, *Ge-stell* and *Gefahr* belong to the abyss of *Ereignis*, a distinguished mode of seeing in a constellation of absence and presence. In posthermeneutic distractions, filming is drawn to *Ereignis* as *eignende Eräugnis*.[31] Accordingly, Heidegger grants to thinking "a certain theoretical authority of vision" (*M*, 72), which filming as it occurs in this text will attempt to dispel.

Paradoxically, filming is more and less than *der Wesensblick* of being. It is less because it relates to the "essential" glance of glances while de-lighting being; it is more than an imaginal disclosure in that it disrupts ("films") "imagocentrism," opting for a reflection beyond images and appearances. Thus, filming crystallizes a new turn to *Eräugnis*, a filmic mode of *Gelassenheit* in which the shadow of the end of man will extend "itself out into a space withdrawn from representation" (*QT*, 136). As can readily be seen, the discontinuity of the Heideggerian text lies precisely in Heidegger's own supplementary reading of the historic inscription of being, notably, in the constellation of enframing and danger: "But where danger is, grows the saving power also" (*QT*, 28).

An "imaginal" turning in being makes possible the *Lichtung* of "an as yet uncomprehended form of the gigantic" (*QT*, 153), a radical trembling that can only come from filming. Without presuming to advance a new epistemic order, filming decomposes the dialectic "ends of man" and shows an imaginal alterity within being's transition to a terrain far from the *principium rationis sufficientis*. Relatedly, filming attempts to surpass Heidegger's alterity of infinitely displaced imaginal formations of a self directed toward a "flowing" imagination.[32]

What thinking (i.e., filming) is called upon to think (film) can no longer be thought (filmed) in a purely theoretical or practical vein, at least not to the extent to which thinking is related to a fading of presence and absence. Thus, in a postmodern epoch, the relation of thinking and filming may be grasped as a gathering of images not wedded to a representational experience (*Erlebnis*) of imagination. The difference filming evokes dissipates the self-presence of a dialectically confined imagination. Teleologic images *more metaphysico* withdraw as imagination lights up in the turning of danger.

A "sudden self-lighting" (*jähe Sichlichten*) is contained in this "play of occlusion." Man is seen as withdrawing into an ob-scene world of dispersive images. World may exceed "its" image (*Bild*). "And so we find philosophy falling asleep once more: this time not the sleep of dogmatism, but that of anthropology" (*OT*, 341). From the vantage point of "the end of philosophy," it could be said that filming awakens thought from such sleep and that this awakening (i.e., filming) occurs in the very uprooting of anthropology and subjectivity. "An imminent new form of thought" (*OT*, 342) is announced: imagination's terrain of "geneafilmic" judgment.

In conclusion, it should be recognized that images of difference revealed in contemporary thought lack the metaphysical crudity that satisfies the desire of self-consciousness. Judgment is free to "measure" the freedom of imagination with regard to a filmic turn of being. This imaginal defloration of epistemic subjectivity marks the sublime movement of imagination, channeling the intuitions, the categories, and the ideas of reason into the diffuse fields of *das Freie des Offenen*. Thinking, exposing "a free opening" of subject, turns its matter to an anticipatory look (*Vor-bild*) of being, notably, to filming, which will shine beyond the specifically specular reflections of our epoch in a de-lighted constellation of imagination and judgment.

3

◆

Velázquez's Glance, Foucault's Smile: A Diacritical Glance at Power

The structure of representation is the very root of the modern order of ground, preceding both high modernity and postmodernism. For Foucault, however, it is a classical root and, paradoxically, one which does not touch the ground of the subject. Indeed, the epistemological space of thinking prior to the apparent decentering of the principle of ground can be regarded as a peculiar interlacing of classical and postmodern elements, especially with regard to the question of representation. In this chapter I endeavor to explain the intrametaphysical "hoverings" of representation in the classical order of power, so as to shed more light on the dissension problem in the modernity-postmodernism debate.

Initially, the matter of Foucault's distinction between the "classical age" and what is generally designated as modernity must be emphasized. The former denotes the epoch of representation; the latter encloses representation within the prioritized power of the subject. Foucault displaces the Heideggerian reading of modern philosophy from Descartes to Nietzsche as a metaphysics of subjectivity. While Foucault does not deny the power of transcendental consciousness in modern thought, he places this epistemic space primarily into the domain of high modernity, that is, into the texts of Kant, Hegel, and Marx. Modernity, which commences with Descartes, conveys a shift from a transcendent representation of ground to the ground of representation. But, for Foucault, "all that remains is representation" (*OT*, 79). Hence, the Cartesian epistemology of the subject does not

40

penetrate representation itself. Descartes, according to Foucault, misunderstands both the classical independence of representation and that of modernity.

By understanding ground from the perspectives of representation without prioritizing a representing subject, Foucault introduces an important dimension into the discussion of the genealogy of modern thought: the idea of "the gap that representation creates for itself" (*OT*, 78), a gap that may serve to show the dissension which postmodernism denotes in its withdrawal from the illusion of ground as subject. Instead of turning solely to Descartes in describing the complexity of the classical order, Foucault implicitly relies upon Spinoza, whose order of representations is not determined by the power of a subject's transcendental gaze but by nature's immanent discourse. Foucault's silence with regard to Spinoza's radically different reading of ground does not detract from his indebtedness to Spinoza, particularly evident in his reflective smile at Velázquez's diacritical glance at the classical order of sameness. Classical episteme, Spinoza's philosophy of nature included, is governed by the belief that the essence of and the relations between things are to be conceived of in the form of a representational order which is free of the dominance of the *ego cogito*.[1] Foucault does not deny the Cartesian presence of subject within representation, but he declines to recognize representation's dependence upon the discursive forces of a subject congruous with rationality. He maintains that a genealogy of representation will raise questions about the Cartesian texture of the subject. Thus, without expressly articulating the issue, Foucault anticipates a displacement of ground from the subjective illusion of the pure domain of reason. In view of the claim that representation is all that remains, the concept of ground remains significant, but only in respect of its extrusion from the principle of reason.

According to Foucault, such an extrusion is already evidenced in the classical age by Velázquez's disseminative opening and critique of representation, as revealed in the painting *Las Meninas*. Thus, in his discussion of *Las Meninas*, Foucault focuses upon a work of art, rather than a philosophical text, of the seventeenth century. Velázquez's work expresses the totality of the classical order more effectively and expansively than Descartes' *Meditationes de prima philosophia*, which concentrates its efforts on a single representative function. For Foucault, the Cartesian intention with its hermeneutic *Wirkungsgeschichte* ("effective history") discolors the classical order of representation, confined as it is to the rigorous space of self-consciousness. In *Las Meninas*, however, representation is shown to be free of the explicit dominance of subjectivity.

A closer look at *Las Meninas* reveals the image of the artist, Velázquez, within the painting itself. The presence of the artist highlights the idea that representation belongs to the work of art rather than to the subject. However, representation may signify several subjects besides the painter: the Infanta Margarita, the maids of honor, the dwarfs, the religious figures, the person in the light who appears to leave, and even, or especially, the companion animal sitting serenely in the foreground. Each of these figures may be viewed as tacitly expressing a desire for "what is noble." Indeed, the representative content of *Las Meninas* is a delicate (altered) image which reveals a longing to preserve the power of classical desire, the sovereignty of the same, whose ground is nobility. Nietzsche's genealogy sketches out a particular facet of the noble order correlative with Velázquez's orientation:

> What is noble? What does the word "noble" still mean to us today? What betrays, what allows one to recognize the noble human being, under this heavy, overcast sky of the beginning rule of the plebs that makes everything opaque and leaden? It is not actions that prove him—actions are always open to many interpretations, always unfathomable—nor is it "works." Among artists and scholars today one finds enough of those who betray by their works, how they are impelled by a profound desire for what is noble; but just this need *for* what is noble is fundamentally different from the needs of the noble soul itself and actually the eloquent and dangerous mark of its lack. It is not the works, it is the *faith* that is decisive here, that determines the order of rank—to take up again an ancient religious formula in a new and more profound sense: some fundamental certainty that a noble soul has about itself, something that cannot be sought, nor found, nor, perhaps, lost. *The noble soul has reverence for itself.* (*BGE*, 227)

Las Meninas unfolds a representation of representation. If subject is to be announced at all, it is representation itself with its polysemous relations, awakening thought to a "new nobility" without allowing thought the power of subject. The painter who appears to look beyond the painting does not gaze at an exterior spectator, who might happen to be a seemingly reflective subject. The arms holding the brush and the palette reveal that he is glancing at his models. We are not the models of the painting, unless we are deemed to be the silhouettes in the center of the canvas. It is clear that the painter is not concerned with a Cartesian spectator of aesthetic reflection. Indeed, in the circle of relations each figure is regarded with classical sameness. Thus, the question of representation emerges from a perspective of order that belies the dominance of a single Cartesian subject as well as the subjective priority of the artist over the work of art. The artist dwells within the work of art as he enhances the nobility of the figures of *Eros* at a distance. While there is no representation *of* ground, there is a sense in which one can say that representation *is* ground, so that, in turn, an apparent impossibility of representing the "act" of representation opens up modes of representation free from the intentionality which, according to Foucault, characterizes the classical mode of thought. The "act" of representing cannot even be appropriated by the one who portrays the representation. Indeed, the painting and not the painter portrays what no subject *per se* represents and what representation names in the classical age: an order of nobility whose mirror-image haunts the spectator as it shines forth indistinctly behind the figures in the painting. It is important for Velazquez to let the spectator glance at the in-finite relation of the figures through the faint image of nobility, within a declining power of presence. This inadvertent fall enables the spectator, then and now, to penetrate the illusion of ground which Velázquez points out in the mirror of the painting. A filmic image of nobility invites the viewer in a postclassical manner to partake in the representative process of portraying a classical mode of being. Velázquez lures the viewer into the classical terrain of the work of art to become one with the artist, the figures, and the imaginal dispersion of nobility.

At first glance, it may seem that the mirror shows little of what is "represented" in the painting. But a closer look reveals Velázquez pointing to an in-finite relation, an invisible region within the representation of the entire work. In the faint mirroring at the very center, this relation reveals the decline of the mimetic order, an erosion of noble ground. It appears that the viewer, even of many generations to come, is invited as a guest, as an aesthetic prelude to what will no longer come into presence, the "logocentric" instrumentality of power. Enframed in the image of the mirror is an eclipse of the order of rank, reflecting the anticipatory mood of the painting. On one view, then, the subtle title of the painting already captures the scene of power falling from presence, not to mention the spectacle of representative configurations appearing as children of an empire fading in the very mirror of its order.

For Velázquez, the order of representation is both visible and invisible. The proximity of either relation, however, becomes problematic as the classical work of representation is drawn into the enframing mirror of a distant epoch. While power falls from the old ground and nobility dissolves, representation itself breaks out of transcendence as the in-finite relation turns to finitude. The silhouettes in this indelible mirror constitute the gap in representation. The otherness of the crown is exemplified not only in the presence of the royal portrait but also in the absence of the king and the figures enchanted by the order of rank. The mimetic presence of nobility collides with the static beauty of a classical order whose reflection turns into the distant glow of a seasoned illusion: a delicate interweaving of an appearing and disappearing power. Both of these relations cast a spell on representation such that one is not entirely certain what actually captivates the figures in the painting. Is it the art of power or the flight from nobility that determines the serene dance of representation? Such a question must be further considered.

A precarious but noble *mimesis* forms the unity of the representative functions of the painting between artist, figures, models, and viewer: the portrait of Philip IV and his young wife, Marianna of Austria, whose image at the center of the art work recedes and decenters representation. The spectator, who is unable to see the front of the canvas in the painting, can still reflect upon the source of the figures' attention, the actual *Vorstellung* ("representation") of the two sovereigns. Between the spectator and the sovereign eye there exists a much greater distance than that of the subjects in the painting and the crown that shines upon the painter. And yet, a trace of permanent change in the classical order is already written on the faces of the subjects, falling from the sublime elegance of noble representation. In the words of Foucault: "The entire picture is looking out at a scene for which it is itself a scene" (*OT*, 14).

Foucault does not thematize the open scene of Velázquez's thought. Instead, he speculates on the "dispersion" of a work whose art "offers itself as representation in its pure form" (*OT*, 16). Without addressing the question of the visitor, who appears for a brief moment in the clearing of the work's configurations, Foucault notes the key issue in Velázquez's painting: "the necessary disappearance of that which is its foundation" (*OT*, 16). In the end, the subject *of* representation becomes a subject *in* representation. Decentering the aesthetic ego, Velázquez introduces an alluring interaction between *eye* and *representation*. The dialectic of master and servant is shattered in a non-hierarchical constellation of subject and representation. Pointing beyond a momentary lapse of power, the painting gains an avenue of entry into high modernity and postmodernism alike.[2]

By the same token, Velázquez guides the viewer to a certain opening in thought, in which representation as concentrated on a single moment, an instance of reflection, disrupts the aristocratic elegance of sameness. It may be that the visitor signifies Velázquez's attempt to withdraw from the painting, indeed, from the power of art, the classical comfort of security, that rational sleep of identity. Eyes look at the sovereign eyes, as a nobleman about to leave his order of rank glances back to the scene from the lighted doorway. On the left side near the back door, a prose of aesthetic light appears in the foreground and in the mirroring center of representation. The hands of the sovereign subjects are not visible; indeed, the hands of all the figures are rather indistinct. From each side of the painting there emerges an "essential void," "a necessary disappearance" of something so real that it has almost become surreal in history. We are faced with a visitor struck by the dream of pure nobility and the cross of Santiago shown on the painter, a self-portrait of Velázquez.[3] While Velázquez extrudes art from the political reality of the palace, another "palace" illuminates the representative order of the painting: that of "dispersion," or the "essential void." An illusive moment emerges in representation: the look or *phainesthai* of a question, a strife within representation, a radical straying from its power. The visitor denotes this look or *phainesthai*; the cross points to filmic transcendence.

For a brief moment, representation accords the concentrated image of nobility's appearance and disappearance. Velázquez arrests this ambivalence with the sublime grace of each figure's still glances. All the lips are sealed, yet they appear to be speaking the same discourse. This sameness signals the representative nature of the classical order, an aesthetic fusion of infinite and finite relations as if a moment in history were to collide with eternity. This mimetic alignment releases representation from the power of identity in its fleeting, discontinuous "movement" toward transcendence. The painting reveals an imaginal dance of difference in which the *eye* plays freely as representation is disengaged from the former order of rank. Relations of power are invariably interrupted by the very movement of representation even in the absence of the intentions of a subject. And so, at last, *Las Meninas* invites a discourse on "dispersion," representation's gap between the power of sameness and the "free play" of difference. The *eye* in *representation* grants the subject as visiting the work of art a terrain in which art resides without the constraints of a mimetic order.

It follows that representation is already dismantled in the representational epoch of the classical order. Velázquez's aesthetic disruption of power opens *Denken* to strategic modalities of discontinuity, subversion, and mimetic de-grounding, none of which presumes to project a new mode of reflective presence. Instead, these strategies point to what has not yet been thematized in a revolutionary genealogy of being. While the beauty of Velázquez's dismasting of *mimesis* continues to shimmer in the strife of modernity and postmodernism, it demystifies the power of representation and provides an intangible yet inevitable link with filming, free of representational anchoring. Accordingly, Foucault's genealogical smile at Velázquez's diacritical glance at power dissolves the seriousness of identity gripped in the historical structure of the principle of ground. In *Les Mots et Les Choses*, Foucault alludes to the subtle valence of Velázquez's tacit mood of thought, whose aesthetic *eye* anticipates what filming is yet to judge:

> To all those who still wish to talk about man, about his reign or his liberation, to all those who still ask themselves questions about what man is in his essence, to all those who wish to take him as their starting-point in

their attempts to reach the truth, to all those who, on the other hand, refer all knowledge back to the truths of man himself, to all those who refuse to formalize without anthropologizing, who refuse to mythologize without demystifying who is thinking, to all these warped and twisted forms of reflection we can answer only with a philosophical laugh—which means, to a certain extent, a silent one. (*OT*, 342–43)

Part Two

◆

AESTHETIC RUPTURES
IN JUDGMENT

4

◆

Adorno's Critique of Pure 'Mimesis'

Filming does not replicate postmodern thought; its genealogy limits the continuum of postmodernism by failing to celebrate the latter's anti-aesthetic of seduction. While it neither affirms nor denies the apparent socio-cultural homogeneity of postmodernism, filming's imaginal terrain of judgment challenges the postmodern fall from aesthetics by means of a new aesthetic force brought to light in Adorno's *Aesthetic Theory*. This textual site of imagination's movement from modernity to postmodernity indicates a transition from a possible critical vantage point of resistance to an indeterminate, nonidentical aesthetic truth. Adorno's text appears as a bridge between two moments of imagination's decisive turn to filming, notably a Kantian "free play" of images and a critical fascination with judgment. Consequently, his path toward art is antinomic. In one sense, aesthetics emerges as a new force that radically questions the departure of the socio-political from the postmodern scene. In another sense, his theory makes possible aesthetic fissures that point to and exceed postmodern operations. As it unfolds a critique of pure *mimesis* without taking the absurd step of signing off from *mimesis* altogether, Adorno's text reveals the inevitable link between modernity and postmodernism.

An aesthetic turn to art in relation to society is no longer determined by a metaphysical, i.e., vertical projection of *mimesis* but rather by imagination's new opening toward a horizontal spacing in which *mimesis*, as it has been conceived, is now rendered inadequate. A new and filmic state of *mimesis* makes Adorno's *Aesthetic Theory* more than just a theory of modernity.[1] Indeed, his deconstruction of *mimesis* through such concepts as "surplus appearance" and "apparition," which we will examine closely, demonstrates the essential difference between Adorno's early "critical theory" (in effect, his negative dialectic, which espouses a modernist pessimism) and his later aesthetic theory, which paves the way for an aesthetic task of thinking in light of the "end of philosophy." Ultimately, *Aesthetic Theory* views modernity from the perspective of a socio-political principle of ground, no matter how displaced or fetishized, and views postmodernism in its inimitable leap from such a ground through unusual aesthetic extensions. The work thus confirms that Adorno's aesthetic is haunted by an inevitable antinomy which cannot be resolved so long as the dialectic remains negative. This antinomy concerns the relation of his foundationalist mode of thought on the side of negative dialectic and his antifoundationalist remarks on the side of aesthetic theory. It is this antinomy, however, which makes a transition from modernity to postmodernity possible. Indeed, Adorno's play of social presence and aesthetic absence functions as a critical strategy for an imagination that sets limits on the interiorized images of modernity as well as the exteriorized images of postmodernity. The antinomy then emerges as a mimetic illusion which falls from a vertical, ground-oriented direction to a horizonal terrain of open spacing. This illusion serves to challenge both the modernist manner of obtaining the social roots of truth and the postmodern attempt to break with socio-historical dimensions of reality. Between the text-milieu of modernity and postmodernism, Adorno demands that thinking address not *die Sache selbst* (there is no matter itself), but rather the matter of "second reflection" with regard to the *Erscheinung* ("appearance") of a work of art.[2] This matter obviates dialectic's "first reflection" or its misuse of the concept of art. In "second reflection" there is a remarkable shift from the dominance of absolute spirit over artworks to an "imaginal free play" without the rule of the concept. Adorno, therefore, regards aesthetics as a new historical force of thought which commences with the question of art in its "social" relation to the work of art.

A NEW AESTHETICS OF 'SECOND REFLECTION'

But can aesthetics be a matter for discussion in a time when art and philosophy seem to be at an end? In a cultural epoch which dwells upon comfort and entertainment, and is seemingly incapable of approaching art outside the mirror of electronic imagery? A change of terrain in aesthetic discourse may commence with a retreat from contemporary modes of "specular" reflection and from conventional texts on aesthetics. Otherwise, questions concerning the relation of art and artworks are unjustifiably restricted to the seduction of a preordained sequence of contemporary images or to narrowly framed concepts of the past. With regard to the latter, aesthetics is witness to the irony of imagination's itinerary within and without the utopia of reason. The risk of losing art in the very *idea* of art, in our reflections on artworks, becomes severe, particularly if reflection turns away from artworks in its attempt to conceptualize them. This is why aesthetics colludes with imagination, even at the risk of falling from reason, in a "geneafilmic" attempt to forge a *theory of works of art* which exceeds a *theory of art*. At this century's end, "a theory of art" may not suffice. In the world of art, where rare and gentle spacings meet what is naturally beautiful, imagination does not turn to the pure region of reason.

Continually challenged by the tension that emerges in the very relation of artworks and art, a new aesthetics cannot be determined by philosophy alone. It must break out of the methodological dominance of a predescribed system of thought. By virtue of its open texture, aesthetics must look ahead to an image of art derived from a *phainesthai* of the concrete work of art. Art must not be regarded as a general order under which artworks are subsumed; similarly, works of art are not particulars which by themselves or in unison constitute art. Nevertheless, while art and artworks differ from each other, they cannot appear without each other. A work of art shows its being in the way it speaks of art, in its shining of art. Here, art refers to a cultural interweaving of society and nature without being the name for a transcendental unity. An artwork points to this interweaving, not as a calculated response to, but as a singular showing of reality. Such a showing needs what Adorno calls "second reflection," that which deflects from *prima philosophia*. Refusing to be guided by received a priori interests, a new aesthetics recognizes that artworks are already reflections of world prior to philosophical reflection. The aesthetic operation of "second reflection" does not confine the reflective mode of imagination to dialectical comprehension. It lets reflection be, in particular the thinking which art and artworks call forth in their distinctive nonidentical relation. In judging works of art, "second reflection" is not derived from reason per se, but from a visional power in art, a power which metaphysics overlooks in subjecting images to pure conceptuality. While the power of art exceeds analysis, it cannot be conceived without it. And yet, how can art as reflection show itself, when a reflection of this showing occurs simultaneously in the very shining of the works of art?

Artworks provide an avenue for disclosing a world which opens reflection anew. This dehiscence of reflection, "a second reflection," so to speak, does not interfere with the artwork's technical shining or *physis*. Only a purely philosophical ("conceptual") aesthetics would obstruct the *Gelassenheit*, or com-posure, of an artwork. This means, of course, that a post-metaphysical aesthetic provides the site for the shining of the artwork and paves the way for the emergence of "truth content" in art. Additionally, such an aesthetic makes possible the meaning of art *through* the work of art. Hence, it makes sense for Adorno to say that works of art need reflection and that art needs aesthetics, not for deciding what art is or what artworks should be, but for guarding the *Gelassenheit* of art so that works of art are not misconceived.

Aesthetics cannot abolish the exchangeability of artworks and the commodification of art in general. Nonetheless, the concrete historical exchange of artworks, embedded in the transactional being of our time, does not prevent aesthetics from pointing out that in spite of the exchange, artworks are free to be what they are. In "second reflection," artworks are free of the hegemonic power of exchange manifested in the commodified form of their external appearance in a museum, gallery, or any other corporate institution. Aesthetics does not submit to the powers that be. In turn, its task is to reveal art as "*imago* of the unexchangeable,"[3] a discourse peculiar to the image of the beautiful in nature. Such a discourse need not confine aesthetic matter to the infrastructural realm of subjectivity. Discourse, for Adorno, is the artistic will of nature (*ein Kunstwollen*), a will to power which speaks ("shows") the image of what is naturally beautiful prior to its assimilation to the principle of ground as (second) nature. Yet, while (first) nature cannot satisfy its desire, art makes it possible for nature to reveal its imaginal "will" through aesthetic discourse. Indeed, this peculiar ability to speak by means of a work of art belongs to the alterity of art, consistently manifested in the com-posure of artworks. Accordingly, aesthetics that is no longer chiefly Kantian, Hegelian, or dialectical in a positive sense places art in the context of world and world in the context of imagination. The work of *imago*, however, is not exposed as production of commodities but as aesthetic reflection accommodating works of art, which are seen as moments of imagination's shining autonomy. Thus, aesthetic theory points to a decisive transformation of imagination and yields a disjunctive, nonnecessary image of art. This image is not a mere picture of the world, a mere *Weltanschauung*, but invariably a radical incision into the process of imagery we are so accustomed to uphold. No mere "romance of practical reason," aesthetics fills the empty screen of the social world with images of appearances exploding into *apparition*, preparing for *promesse du bonheur*. In turning toward images, aesthetics inevitably passes through them in works of art in such a manner as ultimately to be turned away from them. Art as *imago* dispels images of exchange in "second reflection," showing works of art as monadic moments of imagination freed from the secured spaces of identity. After Auschwitz, these new aesthetic moments of *imago* belong to *apparition* in an unexchangeable epoch.

DE-ONTOLOGIZING AESTHETICS

More should be said about Adorno's strategy of "second reflection," especially in connection with the idea of art's withdrawal from being. Adorno deontologizes aesthetics by bringing to light the essential noncompletion of artworks. An artwork is not a work of being but a moment of becoming (*immer wird, nie ist*). There is no eternal quality in the work such that history can claim it will be a work of art forever. What is infinite in art is the work in its finite showing, its socio-historical *phainesthai*. Thus, the image of art revealed in the work is of an entirely different kind than the image of things expressing being. With no essence per se, artworks are not embedded in ontology. They are merely moments of determinate negation passing into monadic moments of thought. It is important to see that art's withdrawal from being, which is simultaneously imagination's breaking through ontology, amounts to an aesthetic disruption of German Idealism and a dissolution of aesthetic categories in general. According to Adorno, aesthetics releases art from Platonic teleo-ontology and reflects upon the artwork's independence from a cramped conception of reason.

An "immanent dynamic" of art can be traced to a compelling noncompleteness of expression in the artwork's continuous *phainesthai* of reification. In Adorno's text, reification is a complex concept which, in short, signifies presence, notably social presence. Here presence is not only regarded in a commodity context but also as waiting for the negation of this context. Negation is always present. Thus, artworks defy being and point perforce to the necessity of no longer rendering presence ontologically. Adorno's text confirms that aesthetics indicates a philosophy of presence obverse to being. But is Adorno's claim burdened by a hermeneutic-materialist reading of being as reification? What is the criterion for judging that being as a socio-theoretic construct is reification? And that social reality is reifying while works of art reflect this reification?

For Adorno, philosophy does not provide magic formulas for addressing the totality of existence. In fact, it questions existence from the perspective of totality, identity, or any other narrowly framed explication. He insists that the work of art, notably its shining texture of openness, makes it possible to disengage the imaginal relations of art from the rigid principle of identity. Even after Auschwitz, the work of art awakens a new sensibility of difference, a dynamic freeing of the human senses.[4] While art does not belong to the essence of being, it participates in the determinate negation of this essence. This negation lies in the artwork's very becoming, in its monadic presence. But "the assertion that artworks are monadic in character is as true as it is problematic" (*AT*, 258). Here, a monadic work of art is not determined by formed modes of *mimesis* but by the aesthetic power of negating being. As it is opened up to aesthetic imagination, the work of art as monad exposes an imaginal spirit without evoking the restrictive assumptions of an absolute frame of reference. Indeed, works of art deflect the concept from absolute spirit. As monadic historical presencing, spirit, which no longer imposes itself on art, waits for reflection's "second nature." This waiting, however, does not occur in a phenomenology of spirit but in an aesthetic experience in which artworks disrupt their alliance with being and indicate a monadic shining toward a new universal by virtue of their particularity. This Adornoian turn renders "phenomenology" capable of pursuing an entirely different image of *Geist* than that of Hegel's *Phänomenologie*.

A STRAYING OF 'MIMESIS'

"To live is to defend a form."[5] Genealogy of form is invariably aligned to the history of *mimesis*. It names what comprises and surpasses imitation. Form is emulation, an intense rivalling of whatever is imitated. In one sense, emulation is a hermeneutics of metaphysics, a dialectic of *mimesis*, mimetic forces at play in art. In another sense, emulation exceeds imitation of *eidos*, and overturns Platonism and German Idealism. Not merely a link in the metaphysical chain of connected ideas, emulation "in action" is a "series of concentric circles reflecting and rivalling one another" (*OT*, 21), traversing the spaces of history and nature in the presence of a dialectic mirror of reflection. All things seem to be able to answer one another. Foucault remarks: "The relation of emulation enables things to imitate one another from one end of the universe to the other without connection or proximity" (*OT*, 19). This non-connective idea of *mimesis* can also be discerned in Adorno's "nonidentical" reading of art. The resemblance between Foucault's notion of "discontinuity" and Adorno's negation of positivity is striking. Both thinkers advance a conception of *mimesis* that is no longer rooted in linearity and is therefore quite different from the received tradition of western metaphysics. Conventionally, *mimesis* is viewed as emulation of *eidos* in a straight chain of concepts from Plato to Husserl. Adorno and Foucault question this single onto-historical dimension of *mimesis*. For them, *mimesis* bespeaks wondrous confrontations of resemblances, none of which is narrowed to a primary ground or framework. Only discontinuous, nonidentical emulations attend to the mimetic activity. While *mimesis* continues to haunt Adorno's aesthetics as well as Foucault's genealogy, the question of the mimetic circle is not addressed explicitly in either philosophy.[6] There always lingers, it seems, a *phainesthai* of the infinite mirror of reflection, a transparent foundation of metaphysics, a heavy glass of gravity that has now been shattered by postmodernism. Mimetic thinking invariably leads to a praxeological dimension. The emulation of *eidos* descends from the abstract beauty of reason to the alienating conditions of a social context. Thus, philosophy virtually signifies the eternal return of the same—the mimetic circle of reason. And theories concerning art and artworks envelop the circle to which the aesthetic categories are confined. The paradox of aesthetics is henceforth closely connected to the problem of *mimesis*.

But can we ever relinquish *mimesis*? What is left of Platonism, marxism, and democracy without emulation? Can this question even be examined from a philosophical perspective? Has there ever been a philosophy which succeeded in occluding *mimesis*? Even imitation of imitation, what Hegel calls "Stoicism," notably, thinking gazing abstractly at thinking itself, even that most imitative process of reflection, imitates something, if only an illusion. But if ground or essence becomes problematic in epistemology and praxeology, what force does *mimesis* have? What is *mimesis* mimetic of? As imagination reaches for an opening which no longer reveals reason as ground, *mimesis* recedes from its origin. Indeed, the crisis of the work of art lies in that very withdrawal—a spacing in which reason is freely at play with imagination. While a vertical notion of *mimesis* is elided, a horizontal *mimesis* opts for a *Nachahmung* ("imitation") which does not measure after an *eidos* or truth. We are granted a reflective com-posure of images, not proto-images of metaphysical anticipation, but images turning from themselves, against themselves, withdrawing from representation, drawn into an aesthetic explosion of appearances, what Adorno calls "apparition."

While not vertical, aesthetics is nonetheless mimetic on a horizontal level. What is good and/or beautiful in an imaginal constellation of nonidentical form and antinomic social content is still imitated by art. And yet, imitation is not mediated by an absolute understanding of the good or the beautiful. Consequently, Adorno's horizontal connection to *mimesis*, while still belonging to a mimetic theory, is to be distinguished from Plato's dialectic naming of *anamnesis*. Plato's *anamnesis* theory is mimetic insofar as learning is thought to be a kind of remembering, a kind of epistemic imitating of the forms. Plato considers artistic acts of imitation to be a mere play of mimicry. Mimicking what is true is precisely what an unlimited aesthetic play of imagination can achieve. So, while Plato denies whatever stands apart from the truth and whatever is related to fiction, no matter how mimetic, he embraces the mimetological game of the dialectic without deconstructing its illusory dimensions. Adorno discredits Plato's dialectic of identity but retains the mimetic impulse in a dialectic of "second reflection." Unlike Plato, he urges the aesthetic use of *phantasia* for the purpose of showing that social domination need not be reality per se. Artworks, then, are the showing-shining of negative *mimesis*. There is no more final positive *mimesis*. Hence the desire for "illusion in art [which] is the attempt to escape from the principle [of reification]" (*AT*, 193). If reification can be diminished or unnerved, art is free to indulge in as many plays of illusion as artists desire.[7] Nevertheless, art does not exist for art's sake but is always swayed by a mimetic value. The mimetic adaptation in art consists of moments, horizontal instances of phantasy's interplay of content and form. According to Adorno, *mimesis* brings the work of art closer to social reality, since art imitates the current character of society as well as what society is not—the image of the beauty of nature. In a double sense, then, art is conjoined with something other than the work of art, namely, society and nature. An aesthetic interlacing of the social and the imaginal serves to unite art and reality without yielding to identity. We will now turn to this complex mimetic undertaking.[8]

A 'MIMESIS' OF TECHNICAL 'EREIGNIS'

Are there genuine aesthetic considerations in Adorno's theory? Or are the aesthetic and the political so interwoven that one misconceives the other? Does Adorno see truth in art solely from the perspectives of a political discourse, notably, that of a new democratic identity? Does his transformation of the mimetic enterprise pave the way for a new political opening, one in which a social life without fear is possible?

What follows will be brief. Adorno is in search of an aesthetic form able to express the prevailing mode of productive forces. These are, first, relations of production in a given historical situation, denoting a complex web of political, technical, and infrastructural interests. Secondly, these material forces are aligned to aesthetic forces of production, which are determined particularly by those of technology, as evidenced in Benjamin's allusions to photography and film. This resolutely modern orientation, namely, that art has a historical core, expressly in its internal elaboration of the material forces of production, indicates that aesthetic theory is simultaneously, but not only, a theory of modernity. This marks an artwork's spontaneous relation to its epoch, a relation of technical *Ereignis*.

Adorno underlines the importance of technical *Ereignis*. Indeed, he equates *Ereignisse* with modernity in art. The inventions of material production are not merely casual mental associations, they "touch on something quite fundamental" (*AT*, 50). The work of imagination appropriates the essence of technique in its mimetic expression of form. Any work of art which presumes to extricate itself from the sophisticated technical procedures of its time does not speak to its time. Here Adorno is critical of Kant's intersubjective concept of morality, which, in its immanent elegance, is thoroughly determined by purity of the will. Technology negates the triumph of such purity and shows that experience is not a pure reserve of the subject. There is no transcendental subject guiding the operations of art. Pure *mimesis* is not acceptable after Auschwitz.

The aesthetic transformation from purity of form to a wealth of sociocultural content is shown in the artwork's spontaneous reaction to its epoch. In literature, the transformation begins with an aesthetic turn to adventure, "the glaring ray of fascination" (*P*, 246). Dislodging the identity of western consciousness, present in technology and capitalism for hundreds of years, literature evokes a reading of texts that takes note of the aesthetic and material conditions of productive forces. These may agitate the reader to a point where she fears that "the narrative will shoot towards [her] like a locomotive in a three-dimensional film" (*P*, 246). It would be inadequate to judge a work of art solely according to the philosophical views of the artist, or simply according to a general *speculum mentis*. "Were this so," Adorno writes, "the work of art would be stillborn; it would exhaust itself in what it says and would not unfold itself in time" (*P*, 247). The aesthetic transformation from purity of form to technical *Ereignis* eviscerates the traditional power of *mimesis*.

It is important to understand this infrastructural transposition of aesthetics without replicating Benjamin's excessive sense of technical *mimesis*. In Adorno's words: "The substantive moment of modern art derives its vehemence from the outside world. The most advanced processes of production, technological and organizational, do not remain confined to the field where they originate" (*AT*, 50). The socio-historical *phainesthai* is not merely a showing in itself; it is a showing *of* subject *away* from subject. Ruptures of the self projected by the essence of technique flow into the aesthetic production of literary works of art. The truth content of Beckett's work, for one, does not originate from a dialectic of purity but from a world of things. Identity, origin of *mimesis*, the unconditional are all notions of reconciliation which real life denies. Art cannot point to what has never existed, unless it first shows what does exist. Its new mimetic activity occurs somewhere between the present and the future. The content of the present, therefore, is shown in the form of the artwork, a form which may present itself in diverse ways in Beckett's plays, in Kafka's novels, or in Proust's *A la Recherche du temps perdu*. How it comes to presence differs from artist to artist and from work to work. Yet in each aesthetic production there appears a strong sense of impenetrability, a sense of darkness, a *glissement* of the signified. Adorno speaks here of the *methexis* of art in the obscure, a participation in the inevitable ambivalence of form which lies somewhere between technical *Ereignis* and a historical "promise that is constantly being broken" (*AT*, 196).

A New Mimetic Strife

A *mimesis* of technical *Ereignis* without the conventional privilege of the subject is closely related to what Adorno calls the new. "The new," he writes, "is necessarily abstract."[9] And art embraces the new in all of its forms, in what cannot be calculated, defined, predecided, or formed in a definite way. Art opens its work to the unknown, to what Adorno calls "the *hidden telos*, a taste for nothing" (*AT*, 32). The artwork reveals the catastrophe of meaning upon which appearance itself becomes abstract. No single, privileged category suffices to judge the "essence" of art, not even form. In its abstraction, art is the social antithesis of reality. Aesthetic distancing, however, does not exclude representation. It signifies a new quality of representation in which the subject silently slips away, falling from power. What remains in the aesthetic circuit of the artwork's shining is the power of abstraction: the tension that aesthetic defiance brings to the scene. "Every human being stands beneath his own dome of heaven" is not merely a painting by Anselm Kiefer; it is a challenge for judgment, evoking at once the presence and absence of a *telos*. The discourse that can be heard in glancing at the painting becomes silent as the image advances beyond its sigetic message. After Auschwitz there can be no place for a self except through a selfless "representation," through an abstraction of withdrawal. Any attempt to read a collective feeling, social or political, into a representation of the subject leaves representation itself behind.[10] The new continues the strife of representation without a dialectic split of subject and object. In Velázquez's work of art, for example, the new is representation at its limit, shown through the graceful exit of the visitor. The power of Velázquez's art lies in its unlimited representational play. Anyone can visit (*visitare*) the site of the new, anyone can see representation without the order of nobility. Adorno's aesthetic reflection appears to us in the figure of the visitor drawn into the light of abstraction: a theory within representation exposing the truth of the painting without enframing the subject. Perhaps the representation is about to exceed its appearance as it becomes "apparition." Ortega y Gasset notes the paradox of Velázquez's text: "The appearance of a thing is its apparition, that moment of reality which consists in its direct presentation to us."[11] But what appears to us so directly is precisely what is new—"the overturning, the *Umschlag*, the *metabole*," the "pure image" of order withdrawing from all objects of the senses in general. What is new is not so much Foucault's smile or Adorno's discomfort, but a sense of seeing or filming which exceeds the power of *mimesis*, "that under which and at which we are thrown, by which we are benumbed and overtaken, the overwhelming."[12] There appears a *Kehre*, a way of thinking which does not keep us locked in limited and limiting modalities of *mimesis*. It is important, therefore, to make the attempt to think filming beyond films and images. The unique eye of imagination, which from Velázquez's *Las Meninas* to Adorno's *Ästhetische Theorie* no longer glances at the ingrained habits of representational thinking, thinks by finer than dialectic means the significance of a disruptive opening of judgment (*Ur-teil*).

5

◆

The Aesthetic Fall
of Political Modernity

In this chapter I want to venture the claim of marxism's end from the perspectives of Adorno's aesthetic theory and today's postmodern climate.[1] For now, I will assume that marxism signifies the climax of political modernity and that its fall disrupts the contemporary cultural scene, which may be described as postmodern only insofar as it points to minimal socio-political self-identity. I will show that the fading of subject, which is readily discernible in the cultural contours of our epoch, constitutes an *abyss* for marxist theory. Classic revolutionary intentions are therefore incapacitated. As the revolutionary subject with a political will to change the social infrastructure evaporates, so does the conventional theory-practice polarity. Hence the question: Shall marxism be able to relate to the subversion of western culture without fading from the scene in a "time without spirit" (*Zeit ohne Geist*)?

While the ob-scenity of our age may reflect the absence of political and moral accountability, postmodern thought neither affirms nor denies this nontransformative propensity. Instead, it highlights that we are free to explore possibilities of change through formative modes of judging. Such modes do not seem to accommodate the principle of political intentionality, making it unlikely for change to come about through narrow political reflections. In consequence, we are faced with the possible end of marxism, not as a dialogical enterprise but at least as a materialist dialectic in the service of a revolutionary system. What may remain of marxism is its hidden genealogy, that "untouched" (second) reflection of capital whose task is neither theoretical nor practical. As indicated earlier, the new task of "second reflection" is to seek a mode of thinking which calls for a "first nature," namely, the image of the beautiful-in-nature.[2] With this aesthetic turn to a tectonic beauty of imagination, marxism begins to challenge the *abyss* of its own theory.

With regard to this challenge, it is necessary to ask what is left of marxism as *social* theory, and what, if anything, is named by a theory without a subject? My own sense is that reification still tarries but that late capitalism may have overturned alienation. In any case, the question concerning the relation of reification to alienation demands some attention. Is there a difference between *Verdinglichung* and *Entfremdung*? Dialectical material-ism fails to emphasize such a distinction as it narrowly searches for the origin of alienation. Without the fanatic orderliness of a revolutionary class concept, marxism faces a dispersed subject sprinkled with socioeconomic immorality: reification fascinates. Ecstatic commodity identity diffuses the postmodern scene. Alienation is denied, but traces of reification are dis-cerned in the technocratic illusionism of private and social modes of pro-duction. Relations of behaving, perceiving, and doing are no longer class oriented. In one sense, commodities please, in another, ideologies satisfy. In both modes, the subject is denaturalized. Postmodernism, at least, celebrates this "nihilism" while it imagines art in capital, and capital in art, a conjunc-tion, precarious primarily to modern reflection, in particular to Hegelian marxism which cannot but see capital as a degenerate form of totalization. Perhaps it is a neo-marxist illusion to continue to insist that a seemingly absolute other called "capital" is concretely accountable for the negative political order. Arguably the origin of alienation lies in an external other, as Marx claims, or in an internal other of bourgeois subjectivity, as Adorno indicates. It seems more plausible, however, to ascribe the origin of aliena-tion to the social interaction of both others. But, then again, it might be more consequential to see that alienation lies in neither, despite Hegel's insight that consciousness as desire necessitates some form of alienation. Marxism cannot afford to cling to the notion of alienation while it disregards precisely what is more preeminent today, namely, the cultural phenomenon of capital's falling from "power" and power's falling from "capital." In brief, such a phenomenon highlights capital's disengagement from a political structure of power, and power's withdrawal from capital as socio-historical substance. This postmodern event exceeds alienation particularly in art, as an aesthetic terrain opens in which art and capital are crystallized. Today, Adorno would mark this event as the death of art, which leaves traces of modernist despair in a fading social consciousness. But surely there is more than one way to read the question of capital's falling and the concomitant filming of power. One can at least refer to the intrametaphysical displace-ments of works of art and commodities, such that capital's withdrawal from its historical signified invites art to be viewed not as reflecting social presence but as reflecting commodity excess. The aesthetic seduction of that post-modern fall may cushion the effects of political and moral indifference. Indeed, it may slide the desires of *homo sapiens* into a network of increased fascination for a commodified, Dionysian lifestyle. This electronic transformation of life into style is not alienation but reification. The difference lies in a postmodern displacement of the subject. Reification discerned in late capitalist pleasures, arising from the disruptions in the relation of capital and power, provides marxism with a new agenda. And here, Adorno's genealogy of aesthetics paves the way for a critical reflection of reification. In its desire for *promesse du bonheur*, Adorno's aesthetic theory offers no definite or clever plan of resistance. If anything, it is more of an anti-strategy than a strategy in its newly aesthetic longing (*Sehnsucht*) for *das Naturschöne*.

Adorno insists that the seemingly innocuous concept of the beautiful-in-nature is the "central motif" of art (*AT*, 119). It marks the "free play" of imagination, whose task it is to continually challenge the infrastructural closure of society with its illusory commodity fascination. But does Adorno's peculiar concept reiterate the singular insights of Schelling's *Philosophy of Art*? Are his references to beautiful nature not a step back to German Idealism, more precisely, to romanticism? And, if so, what has marxism to gain and what have we to gain in the wake of postmodern culture?

It is erroneous to think that the matter of *das Naturschöne* should be relegated to an archaic metaphysical, at best poetic, construction. Perhaps something has occurred in the history of the concept of "the beautiful-in-nature" that makes it more appropriate than any other concept in philosophy to awaken thought to the phenomenal variants of a radically different mode of judging. This, at least, is Adorno's claim. And there are several reasons for it that deserve our attention. For one, this concept is a matter of power, notably, the power of imagination to gather together art and society. Adorno understands the power of imagination as a fleeting movement of images, which cannot be entrapped by the dialectical net of reason in the Hegelian sense. To be sure, there is *Bewegung*, there is reflective movement, but without a *noumenon*, without the convention of identity. The concept of beautiful nature is charged with disseminative power precisely because it does not signify nature as object of production (*Aktionsobjekt*) or mere aesthetic contemplation. *Das Naturschöne* is not a particular natural being. Indeed, it is not nature at all. The paradox of Adorno's concept lies in the difference between the concept's modernist function and its postmodern extension. In other words, what is beautiful-in-nature is so uniquely epistemological, that one wonders how it can be shown to resist social repression. And yet, here, in an unanticipated epistemic space, lies the clue to the very significance of this category.

Only another mode of thought, one that radically questions the invariant impositions of rationality, serves to remind us of what has been erased from memory—imagination's own play of origin. At the threshold of imagination, the myth of a nonrepressive prose of life begins. What we have here is an imaginal understanding of a state of freedom that has never found its way into reality. Imagination still retains this myth in memory (*Gedächtnis*) as an aesthetic play of social origin correlative with natural beauty.[3] Where is imagination carried to when it calls upon *das Naturschöne*?

The genealogy of this concept is closely linked to the history of myth, in short, to the untold story of nature, "first nature," prior to its technical appropriation. Here, nature is not seen as object of action, but as "free play" of thought, as evanescent appearance of beauty. Prior to logocentric judgment, the phenomenon of nature emerges as image of something which cannot be replicated by art or metaphysics, because it dissipates as soon as it is actualized. Neither theory nor practice in the conventional sense resolves the social problematic of freedom. Indeed, the very idea of freedom is displaced. To think it can ever find a home in the historical space of reality may be just as absurd as to believe it ever attained reality (*oikos*) in the metaphysical space of *Geist*. Transposed mythically into imagination's formative terrain, freedom is what nature mirrors fleetingly when it reveals the beautiful.[4] Adorno's inscription of the beautiful-in-nature as phenomenon linked to image introduces an epistemology of aesthetics which exceeds modernist limitations, not to mention his own negative dialectic. In effect, the imaginal beauty of nature opens up ways for a new space of reflection, in which imagination's play of mirroring subverts the ontological principle of ground. What is mirrored in imagination's swaying from the prosaic structure of ground to memory is the natural image of the beautiful, which overturns any imaging that lends itself to reification.

Abandoning all reference to the privilege of subject, Adorno's search for a new social theory is guided by a non-repressive image of freedom revealed by the aesthetic power of imagination. This turn to a radically different epistemic space marks a decisive transformation for marxism. While the social context is explored beyond a perspective of historical presence, art is viewed simultaneously as formative thesis and antithesis of social production. Neither is reason subject, nor is society object of a non-necessitarian social theory. A nonidentical constellation of society and reason defines the aesthetic law of form which refines our sense of the imaginal.

What distinguishes a social theory that is enclosed in a frozen dialectic from one which moves toward change is the sporadic, uncertain image of the beautiful-in-nature. Adorno's concept of natural beauty may indicate new possibilities for marxism, for which judgment is not bound to political values in the received sense but relates freely to an imagination testing the formative criteria of a flexible social theory. Insofar as art is its own monad, it does not imitate nature but rather the ephemeral instance of nature, the image of the new, the not-yet, the possible. Thus, the aesthetic law that Adorno inscribes in his theory of society points to a nonidentical, nonrepressive, indeterminate disposition of "first nature," an event prior to being. As appearance, nature's beauty is more than being. ("Erscheinung ist . . . mehr als Daseiendes" [*AT*, 115].) It is, paradoxically, without presence, without existence. In Adorno's words: "Something appears that does not exist" (*AT*, 121). Embedded in beauty, nature in its *Herkunft* cannot be compared to a particular image. What are we to make of this peculiar aesthetic appearance, which appears not to exist? Which shines forth but does not shine at subject or object? Which is neither subject nor object, nor a pure appearing in and by itself? Which appears in such a way that what is not yet and what is possible may someday be? While a "nonimaginal image" emerges as sign of a promise far from the "language of illusory comfort" (*AT*, 109), Adorno's aesthetics proposes a double theory of appearance, one of natural and one of aesthetic beauty.

With regard to Adorno's interplay of appearances, art intensifies the appearing quality of the art work's appearance by imitating the beautiful-in-nature. A surplus of appearance overreaches appearance itself, showing imagination in its most playful state of withdrawal from the principle of ground.[5] This excess of appearance, which advances to apparition, strains the perceptual framework of society such that the spell of late capitalism is greatly diminished. Adorno writes: "The in-itself (*das Ansichsein*) of art is not an imitation of something real but an anticipation of an in-itself yet to come, of an unknown . . ." (*AT*, 114). In turn, an antinomy haunts Adorno's logic of aesthetics. While society is viewed as historical presence, art dissipates that presence by enhancing the appearance-structure of nature. And yet, art is thought to belong to a particular social context. Adorno's preliminary postmodern disruption of epistemology does not vitiate his modernist, neo-marxist conception of society as alienation. I believe Adorno does not accentuate the difference between alienation and reification, but conceives of the aesthetic project as a challenge to the monolithic structure of the exchange principle. Art succeeds when it shows that it can move outside of presence in its imitation of the beautiful-in-nature. Such mimetic play, however, may not be genuinely disruptive so long as imagination, which makes this play possible, is still relegated to the terrain of bourgeois subjectivity. Even with regard to art, Adorno's genealogy is confined to social presence. Postmodern thought, on the other hand, insists that society be just as much a part of appearance as art. Indeed, the lack of a necessitarian theory of order means that society can be said to be aligned to a purely relational appearance of works of art. Since Adorno thinks of society as the material other or historical essence of appearance, a nonidentical constellation of society and art becomes problematic. Society, regarded from the perspective of an excess of appearance, would have captured the general cultural image of capitalism, enabling Adorno to link the phenomenon of pleasure to the aesthetic play of imagination. Once society is merely seen negatively, the work of art is beautiful primarily in its evisceration of what is socially ugly. Ironically, this "historical" vocation of art tends to extrude the artwork from the possibility of its mimetic task: to become "a cipher of the new, the not-yet, the possible" (*AT*, 109).

The antinomy of Adorno's aesthetic theory is not resolved while society exists essentially outside aesthetic appearance. Adorno realizes that the power of art is the power of society imaged in the very overturning of appearance, and that in the realm of artistic beauty society belongs to the "free play" of this radical overturning.[6] This aesthetic breaking out of appearance, called "apparition," dispels the principle of exchange so substantive for a theory and practice of marxism. Withdrawn from the exchange principle, society can no longer be captured in a theory that strives to establish its historical presence. It can only relate to art that imitates the image that does not exist. Again, Adorno's dialectic cannot come to terms with this antithesis. The historic antagonism of subject and object outside the silent discourse of the beautiful-in-nature speaks differently than the unique postmodern constellation of art and society.

The fertile moment in art, which Adorno calls "apparition," denounces reality (*das Seiende*) and anticipates the end of the exchange principle. Indeed, art is declared as the very image of an unexchangeable world. Still, this aesthetic transformation of German Idealism with its neo-marxist disposition, one that seems at times to be surrealistic, does little to counter the crisis of marxism, even in aesthetic reflection. Adorno's theory flourishes in a unique epistemic space that still depends upon the principle of society's negative presence. The question of marxism's displacement cannot be adequately addressed so long as the difference between art and society is merely *aufgehoben* in an aesthetic space of natural and artistic beauty. The concept of "apparition," which exceeds an aesthetics of images, subverts epistemology by introducing a thinning out, a fading, a filming of being. And yet, beyond the appearances of capital's falling from power and power's falling from capital, an unquestioned a priori of society remains.

Is it possible that Adorno's despair announces itself in art's very overtaking of capital—in an early trace of aesthetic withdrawal of commodities from their "commodity-form"? In some manner, works of art are commodities without commodification. The antagonism of subject and object, of art and society, disappears in capital's falling from power, that is to say, in capital's excessive appearing of the beautiful-in-nature. But is this aesthetic recrudescence the spring of a new metaphysics, the florescence of art beyond the world of things? An initial index of capital's falling from negativity is to be found in Adorno's own reading of the truth of art. He writes: "Art promises what is not real" (*AT*, 122). The imaginary limit of Adorno's horizonal *mimesis* is inscribed in the consistent allusion to "what is not real," which invariably goes back to the suffering that is real, unaccommodating the pleasure that is neither real nor unreal but rather "apparitional." Nonetheless, Adorno's negative dialectic does not resolve the antinomy of aesthetic theory. His reflections on art cannot break the continuum of alienation without the recognition of a filmic dissipation of reification in the sociohistoric terrain of capital. His antifoundationalist strategies fail because he refuses to negate what he claims cannot be negated—the gap between illusion and reality. Presence is therefore reinscribed into his subversive aesthetic critique of ground. In short, his philosophy cannot withdraw from a dialectic of subjectivity.

Still, in the imaginal terrain of Adorno's aesthetic theory, postmodern fissures prevail. "Apparition defies the ruling principle of reality" (*AT*, 122). Here, it seems, he points effectively to a radical opening in which art does not engage the principle of exchange. Indeed, art in the form of a nonessentialist shining or apparition is revealed as "the *imago* of the unexchangeable" (*AT*, 123). But on closer examination of this aesthetic shift, *mimesis* continues and the horizon of its imitability points to the vertical reflection of a world of exchangeable things. Since Adorno refuses to acknowledge the "apparition" of social presence and delights in continually affirming the "repressive hypothesis" of capital, the postmodern scene of capital's falling from power eludes him.[7] He argues for "a real world" without demonstrating how this can be read in a time when reading has fallen into filming, and when filming can be read *without* reading a modernist despair into capital's falling. Beyond Adorno's aesthetic law of form, postmodernism marks the explosion of society as substance. Art and history, dialectic and genealogy, metaphysics and deconstruction belong to the open terrain of appearance, the "free play" of capital. A world without "exchange" is no longer possible, even in the realm of art.[8]

In conclusion, the crisis of marxism belongs to the crisis of reason. Indeed, it is the very crisis of history today. The Hegelian elevation of reason and history has made it difficult for marxism to confront the postmodern scene. It does not know how to relate to a culture whose political signified has withdrawn into the darkness of yesterday's dialectic. How can it cope with a "free play" of imagination challenging reason's sovereignty? What discourse can it provide for a time that no longer avails itself of history as a normative discipline? Drifting in an entirely new space of reflection, marxism finds itself at a turning point. It must decide to exceed its dialectic confinement in a narrow convergence of history and reason. If it is to become theory anew, it must recognize the significance of the contemporary element without imposing a rigid script of the past on society. Marxism fails to understand the disruptive relations of capital and power, inasmuch as it refuses to interpret capital without its signified and power without representation. Marx had no intentions of transforming the dialectic into an invariant and locking it into a political monadology without windows. The question of freedom—social, political, and economic—is peripheral without pointing to a revolutionary transformation of epistemology. Reason must be freed from the interest-accommodations of metaphysics for imagination's new power of transformative judging. In the very tectonic of imagination, reason will attempt to resolve its crisis by overturning negation, its dialectical cutting and severing of the transcendental ground of imagination. Turning from the decadence of a "great *telos*," reason opens itself to the aesthetic law of "free play," to the nonnecessary terrain of art and imagination where marxism may write again. In that postmodern region of disjunctive mirroring, marxism may commence to think capital differently. As reason is freed from the "false necessity" of history, its filmic task will be to free capital from the classic social theory of negative totality. There is more to capital than its alignment with capitalism. The play of filming exceeds the social games of the cities of Dionysos. In the end, the aesthetic law of imagination's "free play" may also subvert postmodernism. And the beauty of nature's image will stand still in memory of an Apollinian discourse that may begin anew with Marx. In this unique space, there is only apparition, "defying us to know what exactly we are looking at," when we see capital as art.[9] At least we can still think of history as a dream, an Apollinian image, as we remember yesterday, when things were still real.

6

❖

Transgressing the Kantian Aesthetic

THE EPISTEMIC TURN

Between Velázquez's diacritical eye and Adorno's aesthetic deframing of marxism, lies Kant's imaginal attempt to question the order of representation. The "step back" to the motif of the *Critique of Judgment* exceeds the radical otherness of modernity by deepening the effects of an epistemic transgression of representation in the concept of judgment "itself." Indeed, Kant's genealogy of imagination, while providing Adorno with the means for a new style of aesthetic theory, harbors the seeds for the postmodern *fleurs du mal* in judgment's "eccentric" turn to filming.

On Kant's argument in the *Critique of Pure Reason*, the concept of representation justifies the division (*Einteilung*) of objects into *phaenomena* and *noumena*. This distinction (of a *mundus sensibilis* and a *mundus intelligibilis*) becomes a matter of great concern in the *Critique of Judgment*. Indeed, there arises, it seems, a peculiar epistemic turn from a phenomenal/noumenal representation of world to an aesthetic presentation of the beautiful in nature. The irony deepens as we glance at this "thing" called "natural beauty," which, in spite of the seemingly subjective judgment of taste, is neither subjective nor objective. Instead, "natural beauty" is called "*a beautiful thing*" (*CJ*, 179). Exceeding the cognitive sense of object and the purely moral sense of purpose, this naturally beautiful "thing" baffles the mind as to its place within the order of representation. Since it is regarded neither as appearance nor as thing-in-itself, but simply as "thing" (*Naturding*), it can be said that Kant's concern in the *Critique of Judgment* is precisely to show that matters of nature and art can be seen independently of judgment's conformity to the principles of cognition and morality. While these matters seem to be appearances, they are judged (*beurteilen*) to be instances of an aesthetic form of purposiveness revealed by a new and distinct power of judgment. As for a work of art, which is thought to be nature's "beautiful representation," the very concept of appearance (*Erscheinung*), in accordance with the Kantian distinction of objects into appearances and things in themselves, becomes problematic once the epistemic difference is attuned to imagination's new "identity," namely, the free aesthetic play of judgment. If the work of art is seen as "beautiful representation" of something naturally beautiful, it is not a mere product of art, so to speak, but a "thing" that is neither a phenomenon nor a noumenon. With regard to this matter, Kant ventures an epistemic turn from a schematic understanding of intuition, which confines imagination to the empirical realm of representation, to a symbolic projection of intuition (*Anschauung*), which frees imagination for a new aesthetic presentation of judgment concomitant with the harmony of the cognitive faculties. In short, the work of art is now seen as a "product" or "matter" (*Sache*) of nature, linked to an aesthetic "identity" between imagination and reflective judgment. This "identity" is disengaged from the framework of ground as conceived by the metaphysical tradition, but is in close proximity to spirit (*Geist*) in judgment's free play with the supersensible, what Kant calls "the matter itself." We are thus dealing with an aesthetic accord of imagination in which judgment reflects freely on the relation of relations, a "grounding" of nature as "the beautiful thing," without a subsumption under the phenomenal-noumenal determinations of subject.

Although Kant does not explicitly articulate the new function of judgment, he is aware that judgment's turn from theoretico-practical reason to an aesthetic movement in imagination "has not been analyzed much so far, even though it very much deserves fuller investigation" (*CJ*, 227). His text is replete with propositions which indicate that the epistemic turn of judgment from determinate, analytic positions is simultaneously an aesthetic turn to imagination's free relation with the cognitive powers. Kant does not develop the relation of imagination's new possibilities of "aesthetic identity" and the question of the "thing," which, when judged to be beautiful, disrupts the representation of the alliance between appearance and the thing itself. In this regard, my concern is to extend Kant's implied approach of opting for an aesthetic skepticism of the theoretical enterprise of *The Critique of Pure Reason*, by outlining the advance made in *The Critique of Judgment* regarding matters of judgment and the "free lawfulness" of imagination.

It will be noticed that Kant proposes an aesthetic theory which brings to light a distinct idea of judging, occasionally named *Beurteilung* (estimation or discrimination) rather than *Urteil* (judgment), which always already precedes works of art so that these may be judged in concert with a free imagination. This peculiar aesthetic antecedence, which metaphysics conceals in its logocentric highlighting of the principle of sufficient reason, reveals that it is not the subject in the work of art that concerns Kant but "nature in the subject" (*CJ*, 175). In turn, cognitive and practical modes of presenting objects are now preceded by a free mode of judging, a pure imaginal operation that gives the rule to aesthetic dimensions, and, in its capacity as taste, views what is judged to be beautiful as universally valid without a definite concept. Contextualizing nature's free play in the subject, imagination opens up as a pure work of art which involves not only a claim to subjective universality but also to disinterestedness, purposiveness, and necessity. For Kant, such a pure work of art reveals a mode of judging (*Beurteilung*) inextricably related to the four moments of the beautiful, and radically different from representational operations of judgment (*Urteil*). I shall briefly consider the transformative possibilities of Kant's aesthetic metaphor of judging the beautiful in its diverse relations.

I begin with the aesthetic moment of pleasure "devoid of all interest," in a filmic art work such as Luis Buñuel's "That Obscure Object of Desire" (1977). Without attending to the imaginal play of sensations constituted by the cinematic texture and coloration of Buñuel's work, we must be wholly indifferent to the technical configurations of the film. Indeed what is beautiful about the film is Buñuel's story of reason's persistent inclination to see imagination from the perspective of representation. Mathieu Fabert signifies reason's desire to reify imagination's play and to turn Conchita, who plays this play, into an "obscure object" of reason's displaced *telos*. Doubtless a remarkable instance of displaying metaphysical power, this film captures the peculiar aesthetic exchange between a mode of judging free for imagination and an imagining free of formed modes of judging. What is at issue, then, is whether or not the presentation of "that obscure object of desire," in its referral to the subject, arouses a feeling of disinterested pleasure. It appears that a *presentation*, quite different from a *representation* of imagination, determines the manner in which the film will be presented to judgment. The seductive collisions of color, design, and texture, which are not excluded from aesthetic judgment, do not by themselves determine whether a film is beautiful or not. Nor should the enticing appearance of Conchita distract from a disinterested discourse on the beautiful, if the imaginal presentations of the film are not cramped by logocentric assumptions. "We can easily see that, in order for me to say that an object is *beautiful*, and to prove that I have taste, what matters is what I do with this presentation within myself, and not the [respect] in which I depend on the object's existence" (*CJ*, 46). For this reason, Kant suggests that we abide in a succession of presentations by means of which we continue the process of aesthetic production, without ever completing a reading of a singular work of art. Furthermore, a work of art will invariably be incomplete within the paradox of imaginal presentations withdrawn from empirical and practical representations. On Kant's view, the work is repeatedly drawn into a disinterested play of imaginal lawfulness linked to the aesthetic purity of taste. In this regard, it seems that the film must gain the approval of a free imagination and be filmed anew according to a spontaneous power of judging, so as to provide free pleasure. Hence, when we look at "That Obscure Object of Desire," we see a film in which Conchita presents "an *other* film," where imagination glides along the wall of subjectivity until reason in its dominance is out of sight. This other film is that which is beautiful in Conchita's own presentation of the "film" in reason. Displacing the initial representation of a particular art work, a succession of presentations crystallizes the contours of the pure work of imagination.

A transposition occurs in the eclectic presentations of Buñuel's film. What is beautiful is not the film as such but rather the filming of Conchita's converging double presentations of a free imagination and a new mode of judging. In turn, taste, which comes to light in a disinterested work of art, collides freely with diverse aesthetic presentations of individual matters of art. Only the aesthetic power of imagination, exceedingly post-ontological in its ability to play freely with the unique presentations of the cognitive faculties, prompts the rise of a pure work of art, continually shaping the presentations of particular art works in the very process of judging something to be beautiful. In imagination's "free play," judgment (*Beurteilung*) may be regarded as the "universal voice" in each work of art, that is, the pure work of art exceeding objective reflection.

What we *ought* to agree on, then, is solely the idea that a work of art is declared to be beautiful not because it is beautiful (nothing is beautiful by itself) but because the pure work of art in the imaginal presentation of a particular work is liked universally. Hence, merely looking at Buñuel's film does not require that everyone consider it beautiful. But reflecting aesthetically on this work demands a universal consensus as to the ascription of the beautiful to the imaginal presentation of that work. "When this happens," Kant writes, "the cognitive powers brought into play by this presentation are in free play, because no determinate concept restricts them to a particular rule of cognition" (*CJ*, 62).

The third moment in a judgment of taste shows purposiveness in relation to the expansion of imaginal presentation. While the presentation of an art work draws the spatial and temporal configurations into purposiveness, that is, into a way of presenting the work amenable to being liked universally, the form of purposiveness does not come into play until we take note of the presentations that can be combined by imagination. "Therefore the liking that, without a concept, we judge to be universally communicable and hence to be the basis that determines a judgment of taste, can be nothing but the subjective purposiveness in the presentation of an object, without any purpose (whether objective or subjective), and hence the mere form of purposiveness, insofar as we are conscious of it, in the presentation by which an object is *given* us" (CJ, 66). Taste is, therefore, founded on (*Bestimmungsgrund*) the pure work of art, an imaginal mirroring, a filming, which serves to provide an individual work of art with the freedom of presentations, so that no presentation is determined either by an objective or subjective purpose. A presentation of the work is always free for a formal purposive way of presenting the work by means of a disinterested "mirror" of imagination. The pure work of art is indeed the awareness of this "mirror," in which an alliance of presentations expresses a free liking for an art work, so that a painting, a poem, and a musical composition can be presented within the purposive connection (*nexus finalis*) of a free imagination.

The open texture in a pure work of art is not without a diffusion of impressions, conveyed in Buñuel's film by the "nakedness [of Conchita's] kisses of linen sheets and silk" (*FM*, 44). Still, purposiveness is rendered inadequate unless it enhances the presentational powers of imagination in exceeding the charms of Conchita's form, within and beyond the film in an unforeseeably new alliance of aesthetic presentations. The pure work of art thus invites other works of art to undergo *Beurteilung*. Whence this film may be enveloped in a poetic discourse by Baudelaire. Indeed, his poem "A Strange Man's Dream" may reveal "that obscure object of desire" initially carried off by reason while seducing judgment without reason's *knowing*. The poem unfolds a space of dispersion, reason's concern for Conchita's diverse itinerary, imagination's free play of purposiveness whose form exhibits countless presentational possibilities. Falling from representation, reason dreams of Conchita:

> Have you felt—I have—a pain that you enjoyed?
> Do they say about you, too: "How strange [she] is!"
> —I was dying, and a special agony
> filled my eager soul: dread and desire,
> anguish and expectation—no sense of revolt.
> The closer I came to what would be the end,
> the sharper was my torment and the more welcome;
> my heart was wrenching free from the usual world.
> I was like a child in front of a stage,
> hating the curtain as if it were in the way . . .
> Finally the cold truth was revealed:
> I had simply died, and the terrible dawn
> enveloped me. Could this be all there is?
> The curtain was up, and I was waiting still.
> (*FM*, 151)

Buñuel's film elides the subject, particularly reason in its opulence and hybris, while "nature in the subject," that is, Conchita's free play of difference, blooms in silent purposiveness. The closer Mathieu Fabert comes to the end of reason's dream, the more Conchita forgets "the house [they] lived in then, it was just outside of town, a little white house . . ." (*FM*, 104). A "white mythology" of desire, whose identity is shattered, keeps the subject waiting still. The "cold truth" of the film reveals the ending of representational relations between imagination and reason, as Conchita and Mathieu Fabert disappear from the scene of desire. Judgment remains: Conchita's furtive force, an *other* woman in imagination, stepping out into the open. Unrelenting, shadows stream out of reason's darkness: What is beautiful in the night leads the film in this poem to a possible presentation in a symphony, in which the fourth movement films "nature in the subject," while the fifth movement of Berlioz's *Symphonie fantastique* might indicate that Mathieu's aesthetic march to the scaffold, possibly the end of the subject, is merely a purposive image in Conchita's free play of imagination. Judgment, effacing semblances of the subject, freely forgets the house imagination lived in then, the *ethos* just outside of Athens. And now, in Paris, reason is much closer to the flowers of evil. "I come and go—the Demon tags along, hanging around me like the air I breathe" (*FM*, 121).

It follows that purposiveness delimits disinterestedness by means of an aesthetic alliance of presentations, ever rupturing judgment as it points to the gulf that separates representation from presentation, the order of interests from the freedom of imagination. Similarly, the metaphoric limitation of disinterestedness through the pure work of art is possible because of the modality of aesthetic pleasure, in a manner of speaking, the necessary relation of the pure work of art and the presentations of art works that are judged to be beautiful. In short, the pure work of art is necessarily linked to the beautiful. A judgment of taste about the beautiful does not maintain that everyone *will* agree but that everyone *ought* to agree that something is beautiful, if it can be shown to be connected to a feeling of pleasure that is necessarily free and purposive, without leaning on a specific purpose. While in the first critique Kant argues that universality and necessity are inseparable from each other, the third critique introduces a conditional relation between the universal and the necessary, a relation that pertains, of course, to the free power of imagination. The peculiarity of this relation lies solely in the aesthetic manner of presenting objects to the subject. This manner is *exemplary* in that the presentation of the object is referred to an "archetypical" dimension in the subject, in which judgment disregards sensory preferences and moral interests. An aesthetic grounding arouses a necessary pleasure if what is declared to be beautiful pertains to a universal and disinterested relation between imagination and the presentational powers of judging (*Beurteilung*). The demand for such a relation, the aesthetic relation, that is, the pure work of art, is necessary in order to show that a work of art elicits a manner of thinking, revealing a radical change in attitude toward being. What follows is necessity, a new quality of pleasure, generated by the aesthetic form of free purposiveness.[1]

AESTHETIC DISRUPTIONS IN JUDGMENT

Kant's text indicates not only a radical transformation of the epistemic difference of phenomenon-noumenon but also a radically different manner (*modus*) of seeing a work of art. Art is not perceived culturally in relation to individual works of art at hand but as works of imagination's free culture, invariably open in a continuous movement of judging. We might say that in the *Critique of Judgment*, Kant exposes the conditions for the possibility of works of art within a framework of aesthetic freedom. Hence, the epistemic leap from the transcendental method of the distinction of ground to an aesthetic manner of seeing, which dissolves this distinction in imaginal free play, opens "a new ground" for judgment and art. Respectively, art needs judgment to be pure, and judgment needs art to be free for the open terrain of imagination. Indeed, judgment and art form a culture of pleasure by means of a pure work of art, which arises in a "supplementary shining" of imagination exceedingly free in its aesthetic play. A peculiar mirroring draws judgment into the imaginal regions of art. In relating to a work of art, judgment now begins to see what it did not see in its dialectical service to understanding—namely, that it *should* be free for imagination. Imagination opens its site for presentational possibilities of every art work.

Simultaneously, imagination is that component in judgment which exceeds the phenomenal-noumenal relations of an object, that is, it divides the ordinary materiality in matters of art from one's perception of art in order to see what matters freely in art. In relation to contemporary culture, seeing art from Kant's perspective of aesthetic judgment is to introduce a dimension of anti-art into aesthetics. There is a correlation between "free purposiveness" and "anti-art," if by anti-art we understand that particular moment in a work of art that is pure. The "content" of imagination's free play reveals this aesthetic correlation.

Withdrawing from a determinate purpose, imagination nevertheless tarries in a purposive manner of playing. Free of teleologic closure, it opens judgment to a form of purposiveness which calls into question the existence of appearances. Kant's epistemological model is in turn supplemented by his peculiar aesthetic enterprise. The *mimesis* of cognition and morality is no longer founded on the idea of the noumenon as the supersensible but rather on a pure work of art which serves to stand in as the "new ground" of judgment. Art reveals that reason imitates imagination in its new search of the supersensible. Kant thus looks at art as mediating what is natural, that is, conceptual, and what is moral. The interests of reason dissolve in the aesthetic disinterestedness of imagination. Still, reason's desire for the infinite is not abandoned. On the contrary, it becomes free for judgment's aesthetic critique, that is, reason descends to imagination in order to become in relation to the pure work of art what it cannot become in relation to the pure work of cognition. *Mimesis* is no longer aligned to the principle of ground but to a "new ground" of reflective judgment, the pure work of art, the primal image (*Ur-bild*) of aesthetic images in which reason, imitating art, strives to discover "itself" anew.

Not simply a matter of judging a particular work of art, art, in the aesthetic form of reason's new *mimesis*, determines the power of free purposiveness in imagination's play with the mental powers. It is important to bear in mind that imagination's play with our mental powers is invariably consistent with judgment's relation to particular works of art. It seems that this correlation is necessary in order to understand Kant's dialectic of aesthetic pleasure and purity. What is pure or free in aesthetic pleasure is precisely what is not the concrete work of art in a work of art, namely, the anti-art. "From now on," Adorno writes, "no art will be conceivable without the moment of anti-art" (*AT*, 43).

Accordingly, we are seeing "free purposiveness" in the supplementary shining of a pure work of art, so that we are invariably challenged by moments of purposiveness in the free imaginal relations between judgment and art. The anti-art, it seems, draws its power of judgment from a concrete work of art, while the latter mirrors its being in the very shining that exceeds its own manifestations. Art is merely a matter of distinct relations, notably the relations of our mental powers and the aesthetic ("anti-art") play of judgment with individual artworks.

On Kant's view, then, art is neither something that primarily happens in the history of art or in contemporary culture, nor merely the product of a subjective aesthetics, since such an aesthetics is precisely what Kant questions in a text which lets judgment decide freely. Art is essentially a "schema of imagination," which relates the mental faculties to particular works of art without integrating their objective existence into aesthetic judgment. As semblance of the universal (that is, not given), art (resembling nature, notably the beauty of nature) serves as "primal image" of imagination, which judgment relates to a natural thing or a particular work of art. So, even though judgment correlates the pure work of art (imagination's free play) with matters of art in particular, art is not extracted from reflective judgment. On the contrary, judgment merely highlights what imagination produces in its pure and free play of relations. To designate Kant's aesthetics primarily as subjective is to misconstrue the aesthetic and teleologic role of imagination in the *Critique of Judgment*. Subsumption of art under the subject, or subsumption in general, is not the task of the third critique. Instead, we note disruptions of judgment's subjective dominance over imagination. While it is possible to disengage art from a logocentric subsumption, it is not possible to detach art from imagination.

What matters is not the nature of art itself, nor even that of judgment in general, but rather *how* art and judgment are integrated in the aesthetic play of imagination. This question is most important when one considers Kant's emphasis on the relation of judgment and culture. Throughout the *Critique of Judgment*, Kant unfolds his unique conception of judgment in accordance with the aesthetic propensity of the subject for culture. What emerges as the thread that binds art and judgment is a very distinct idea of culture. Again, culture is not merely what is historically given as society to date but nature's ultimate purpose in imagination. It is, one might say, imagination's genial activity, its free purposiveness without falling into a moral order. Culture corresponds to a play of forms in which teleological moments of judgment are presented without establishing teleological structures. This can be done best if culture is grasped as "producing in a rational being an aptitude for purposes generally" (*CJ*, 319), in a manner that frees imagination. Only the culture of a pure work of art, of a certain aesthetic ideal, which simultaneously expresses the freedom of imagination, is universally communicable in judgment's relation to a particular work of art. The mental powers must be exposed to a form of purposiveness that combines both art and judgment in reflective interplay, while exposing qualities which "constitute the sociability that befits humanity and distinguishes it from the limitation of animals" (*CJ*, 231).

The subjective/objective debate about art disregards not only the epistemic turn in Kant's aesthetics but also, and, perhaps, more importantly, the manner in which culture is shown to be the anti-art in art. As propensity for "free purposiveness," culture sets out to free art for what is not art in an indelible play of judgment. It may be more correct to say that judgment is the moment of anti-art in art, especially in its attribution of the beauty of nature to matters of art. Art may therefore have to go beyond what appears in works of art in order to be judged. The indefinite concept that lies at the basis of its "primal image" may very well be the anti-art of judgment. Thus, art has no power of resistance without "free purposiveness," conceived in the form of a momentary relation between judgment and a singular work of art. That momentary relation compares a work of art to the culture of anti-art, that is, to Kant's *Critique of Judgment*, without confining art to a domain of meaning constituted by subjectivity.

JUDGMENT'S 'ECCENTRIC COURSE'

For Kant, "among all the arts *poetry* holds the highest rank" (*CJ*, 196). Its distinctive play with illusion, its pursuit of the presentational powers of imagination, exhibits the primacy of aesthetic purity. Expressing the disjunction of judgment and reflection, poetry emerges as a "different *ethos*," a new aesthetic place for the pure work of art. Attuning the spirit to ideas, poetry signifies the play of plays, a primordial presentation of imagination, continually attending to the split, the gap, the post-aesthetic madness of free purposiveness. Poetry lets thinking be open to guidance by imagination, offering judgment an unlimited variety of possible forms of purposiveness. Without assuming an underlying intention, poetry is the inner motion of the pure work of art, the beginning of judgment's play with aesthetic disinterestedness. Ironically, it may be thought of as a "serene contemplation" of imagination playing within the eruption of the power of judgment. Exhibiting judgment's withdrawal from metaphysical comfort, poetry ventures on its "eccentric course" of thought toward a home (*Heimat*) without ground, revealing the seductive tension of reason's severance from the order of representation. While embracing the silence of reason's dissension, poetry sets the tone for a metaphysical end of judgment and the beginning of a unique aesthetic economy of doubt. At a loss for words to express the privileged domain of certainty, judging can neither speak nor write of "itself." In the unique domain of poetic freedom, there is no "essence" in judgment (*Urteilskraft*). There are only modalities of judging which conjoin the aesthetic relations of the beautiful in accordance with the inevitable withdrawal from delimited interests of representation. Without its habitual order, reason, thrown from absolute totality into a post-dialectic madness, has limited control over the unlimited possibility of aesthetic ideas.

Poetry, radically displacing reason, plays with the pure work of art, imagination's free exchange without moral investments. In strange complicity with the Kantian text, Hölderlin's late poetry expands the subversion of identity in moments of doubting the profundity of metaphysics. Judgment, falling from *ethos*, meets the demon of disinterestedness in a poetic discourse which Hölderlin names "In Lovely Blueness . . ." (*In Lieblicher Bläue*).

> In lovely blueness with its metal roof the steeple blossoms. Around it the crying of swallows hovers, most moving blueness surrounds it. The sun hangs high above it and colors the sheets of tin . . . If now someone comes down beneath the bell, comes down those steps, a still life it is, because, when the figure is so detached, man's imagery [*Bildsamkeit*] is brought out . . . But purity too is beauty. Within, out of difference a serious spirit [*Geist*] is formed. Yet these images are so simple, so very holy are they, that indeed often one is afraid to describe them. As long as kindness, which is pure, remains in his heart not unhappily a man may compare

himself with the divine. Is God unknown? Is he manifest as the sky? This rather I believe. It is the measure of man. Full of merit, still poetically, man dwells on this earth. But the darkness of night with all the stars is not purer, if I could put it like that, than man, who is called an image of the gods [*Gottheit*].

Is there a measure on earth? There is none. For never the creator's worlds constrict the progress of thunder. A flower too is beautiful, because it blooms under the sun. Often in life the eye discovers beings that could be called much more beautiful still than flowers. Oh, well, I know it! For to bleed in form [*Gestalt*] and heart, and wholly to be no more, does that please God? (*PF*, 601–03)

Hölderlin's poem exposes a judging that gazes at the mirrorless "image" of a free imagination without the support of a measuring ground. It declares the difficulty of naming the aesthetic disorder of reason, the astonishing silence of being. Discerning a different project, poetic discourse reveals an excess of taste in each moment (*Augenblick*) of judgment's openness for a seemingly inaccessible purity. The relations of the beautiful wither in the wind that blows against the flowers of a divine terrain. Exiled from the image of the gods, judgment begins to wander aimlessly in the non-way of disinterestedness. Without a measure on earth, it dwells poetically in the ceaseless framing of beauty's withdrawal from images of the sensible and the supersensible.

Discerning the relations of taste which no longer connect purposiveness to a specific purpose, judgment uncovers something more beautiful than reason's role as master of the house of being. "Within [purity], out of difference . . . spirit is formed" (*PF*, 601). And, for Hölderlin, philosophy cannot exceed the paradox of judging, that poetic play with "images" so simple that "one is often afraid to describe them" (*PF*, 601). "Oh, well, I know it," Hölderlin writes: "For to bleed in form and heart, and wholly to be no more, does that please God?" (*PF*, 601). For as long as judgment remains pure, disinterestedness is freely beautiful. Though the form of purposiveness is now without essence, the purposiveness of form is still a poetic dwelling. What comes over thought, as it ponders too much of the unspeakable withdrawal of the supersensible, is an "eccentric course," an abysmal turn, yet, a beautiful site for thinking. "Would I like to be a comet?" Hölderlin asks. "I think so. For they possess the swiftness of birds; they blossom with fire and are like children in purity" (*PF*, 603). To desire more than that, he claims, judgment cannot presume. Like children in purity, the presentational powers of imagination play without concepts in the beauty of judgment's poetic dwelling.

JUDGMENT'S SUBLIME DISINTERESTEDNESS

Exceeding the Kantian text, judgment is ever free to exit the transcendental region of taste in its aesthetic openness to radical disinterestedness. Reaching out toward imaginal free play, it simultaneously withdraws from the teleologic confines presented in the *Critique of Judgment*. In its sublime chaos, *Beurteilung* shatters the free purposiveness of the beautiful, while it consistently deconstructs representation. Even reason's metaphysical desire fades into disinterestedness as judgment, facing pure relations of inaccessible freedom, is released to filming, a post-imaginal play in thought ever ready to think (as Conchita does) what is neither solely phenomenal nor noumenal. While a Hegelian leap is tempting, judgment cannot "mirror" *itself* in the absence of essence and truth. Straying into sublimity, judging emerges as a pure post-aesthetic relation without the corollaries of judgment itself. Withdrawn, too, from universal communicability and necessity, judging is "its" own free counterpurposiveness, a "Conchitian" turn to radical disinterestedness. Disrupting the aesthetic-teleologic connection of the beautiful, judging now finds filming, a postmodern mode in which the pleasure of imaginal opening is metaphysically without purpose.

A genealogy of filming can be discerned in the disruptive relation of judgment to the four moments of the beautiful. Two of these moments, universality and necessity, dissolve in imagination's free movement toward the "purposiveness" of sublime disinterestedness. While Kant's *Critique of Judgment* opens imagination toward a purposiveness without purpose, reflective aesthetic judgment remains caught in the web of an interest in the supersensible, "since, after all, everything we do with our powers must in the end aim at the practical and unite in it as its goal" (*CJ*, 47). Filming, which unnerves the power of synthesis, draws judging (*Beurteilung*) into a counter-metaphysical ending of interest, withdrawing from the supersensible altogether, without escaping from the "epistemic" abyss (*Ab-grund*) of imagination in its uncanny freedom. Hence, a truly disinterested, sublime liking does not occur until judgment releases universality and necessity from the aesthetic moments of the beautiful as it grants purposiveness the pure pleasure of disinterestedness. Taste, however, extending imagination beyond the restful gaze of reason to the contra-purposive movement of the sublime, does not disappear in the disruptively different appearing of the beautiful.

Although Kant never extends his inquiry of aesthetic judgment into the domain of filming, his concept of the sublime ruptures the transcendental closure of taste. What is beautiful may now be judged in accordance with a filming which no longer sees the image of the beautiful mimetically. In turn, representation falls into sublime disarray. What can no longer be represented is what judgment becomes—a post-aesthetic dis-play of pure "filmic" disinterestedness.

Torn from the aesthetic relations of the beautiful, judgment exceeds the form of purposiveness altogether. In its unlimited voyage to filming, judgment violates not only the order and opulence of reason but also the *aesthetic* freedom of imagination. Baudelaire reveals a sense of judgment's sublime post-Kantian withdrawal into unboundedness in a poem named "A Fantastic Engraving":

> Uncanny apparition—all it wears,
> grotesquely canted on that grinning skull,
> is a garland woven out of worms! No spurs,
> no whip, and still this ghostly cavalier
> urges his apocalyptic nag
> onward till her flaring nostrils bleed,
> horse and horseman mad in pursuit of Space,
> trampling Infinity with reckless hooves!
> The rider brandishes a flaming sword
> above the nameless hordes he gallops down,
> and like a prince inspecting his domain
> quarters that unending graveyard where
> a bleak white sun exposes, mile on mile,
> history's hecatombs, ancient and modern both.
> (*FM*, 72)

Beyond the Kantian space of aesthetic peace, in imagination's free play, judgment moves within the epistemic violence of the sublime. While the *Critique of Judgment* is ultimately indifferent to the radical consequences of disinterestedness and sublimity, Baudelaire highlights judgment's freedom from the imaginal power of aesthetic purposiveness. An "uncanny apparition," judgment inspects an unending and unimaginable domain, while the "bleak white sun" of the pure work of imagination fails to expose the totality of ideas intertwined with the supersensible. Indeed, judgment's turn from "disinterestedness" to the sublime is haunted by a movement at the limits of the imaginal, the vertigo in filming. Dimly glimpsing the rim of judgment, filming unfolds the sublime in its complete withdrawal from purposiveness. The unconditioned never to be met with in experience is also expelled from reason's empire. "Trampling infinity with reckless hooves," judgment dwells poetically with sublime but radiant glances at "old Plato's scowling eyes" (*FM*, 124). Transposed into filming's fervent light, the sublime, more beautiful than aesthetic disinterestedness, advances beyond the Kantian confines of an open imagination. Within the sublime, out of difference, a new mode of judging is formed: a filming drawn toward the chasm, the chaotic eyes of a fleeting imagination. "Upon the instant,

Reason's light went out and darkness shrouded this once-searching mind" named judgment (*FM*, 24).

The poetic spacings of Hölderlin and Baudelaire reveal the sublime as a nonmimetic "mirror" of the beautiful. What is beautiful is formless, helmless, and free: a distinctive, contrapurposive mode of judging. Exceeding the aesthetic form of purposiveness, judgment plunges from the harmonious order of pleasure, while it no longer views the pure work of art through the protective lenses of imagination. Withdrawing swiftly from presence, it defers to the sublime, a post-aesthetic of filming, which captures the pure work of art in fleeting moments of disinterestedness. Taste appears differently; in *another* beginning, it exposes judgment as the anti-art in art precisely in accordance with a filming that concedes unlimited presentations of sublime disruptions. By taking the transcendental exigencies of taste to their logical end, without, however, giving in to the quantitative and modal moments in a judgment about the beautiful, filming opens the discourse of radical disinterestedness to a post-aesthetic and, paradoxically, to a new mimetic strife of judgment.

Part Three

◆

A POST-AESTHETIC
OF FILMING

7

◆

Radical Spacing
in 'Gelassenheit'

Without employing the gerund form of filming in relation to becoming (*Werden*), the Kantian text, most notably, the *Critique of Judgment*, evokes a sense of filming in its aesthetic reference to imagination's "free play" and the sublime. Still, the Kantian text is not free to unfold its "becoming" in order that filming may emerge as a gerundial event. Imagination in its transcendental domain operates primarily as a noun; it does not yet attain the kinetic, verbal economy of Derrida's *writing*, a space where filming is initially released from reason's pure self-presence. Transgressing the Kantian aesthetic, filming, then, radically disrupts not only absolute identity (of identity and difference) but also the nonidentical constellation of inside and outside. This gerundial disruption begins with a perceptibility (*Vernehmbarkeit*) of capital, illuminated here from a perspective of filming in which interiority and exteriority are freed from empirical and metaphysical interconnections. But what, then, commences with filming?

The noun and/or verb from which filming is derived may serve as a clue to the disruptive matter of filming. Its earliest forms relate to the Anglo-Saxon term *filmen*, an extension of the old Teutonic *felmen*, related to the root of *fellen*, whose general sense is "to cause to fall," "to strike down," literally, "to cut down (a tree)," "to fell down." Filming contains a wide range of meanings, but for now it suffices to awaken the sense of "break down, overthrow" in order to highlight its engagement in felling down (striking down) the metaphysical edifice of reason's narrow spacings. With regard to our epoch, filming emerges as a ruptured, chafed, and broken "skin" or image of becoming. This "imaginal" thinness, however, does not diminish the strength of its kinetic force, free from the teleologic determinations of reason. Fading from a rational superiority of metaphysical oppositions, the filmic network exceeds the logocentric "will to power." Filming emerges as a constellation of judgments exceeding the transcendental interplay of cognitive faculties. As an entirely different mode of thinking (*Denken*), it traces the technological contours of an imagination pointing to the outside, without yielding to the dialectic comfort of inside/outside oppositions. There is no cognitive obstinacy to its operation. Dismantling the epistemological priority of subjectivity, filming brings to view the ex-positional transgressions of imagination's play of judging. While it may merely "be" the inscribed surface of events traced by a new mode of judging, its locus of movement surfaces as capital dissipating the pure space of truth.

More than imaging or discerning the hidden meaning of images, filming invariably shoulders the principle of elegance, perhaps the only lasting virtue, which Kant calls—precision. In complicity with the current mood of the sciences, yet quite distinct from the hermeneutic direction, filming ironically exceeds the bold and exact operations of the camera. It is more than a postmodern eye striking out against the Cartesian subject. In chapter 2 I indicated that filming, which allows for exactitude, exceeds the technological interests of filmmaking, the sciences, and the arts. Staging the scene of imagination's "free play," filming transgresses the cultural limitations of the cinema as well as the hermeneutic delimitations of interpretation. Digressing from the subject of ideological identity, filming disengages the hermeneutic urge to see and interpret "things" in a particular way, be it transcendental, absolute, or perspectival. But is it merely a variance of pure *Geist*, perhaps transformed to suit the current historical horizon? Or an inversion of pure reason, an empty, noninterpretive judging gliding freely over the rhythmic waters of "work, rest, and holiday"?[1]

With filming there commences a radical questioning of the dialectic script imposed upon capital by infra/superstructural modes of interpretation. Breaking with this tradition, filming undertakes to expose capital differently. One may venture to say that capital is a *prolepsis* of filming. *Prolepsis*, derived from the Greek words *pro* ("before") and *lambanein* ("to take, to seize"), is an anticipatory movement which seizes representation before it (representation) imposes a metaphysical script upon time, a time that is to come (*Zukunft*).[2] Capital, then, is a proleptic domain within filming, which disrupts the schematic power of images in order to release time from the imaginal. Breaking out of the genealogical space of continuity and discontinuity, capital sets the stage for a thinning out and fading of imaging, while simultaneously providing in advance the "promise" of a radically different time. In brief, capital "takes possession" of the gap subsequent to the filmic lapse and slippage of images. This postmodern seizure of a disjunctive space within imagination transposes imagination into filming, where filming's transformative modes of judging open up ways of seeing untainted by the prosaic relations of our epoch. The delicate texture of this new "epistemic" space effaces the logocentric power of imagination as it clears the way for an open field of judging which dismantles metaphysics' final cast: "the wills to power." An "epistemic" jolt at first, until one ascertains that even "the wills to power" are not things in themselves but mere "emanations" from the surface of capital, drawn into a radically new spacing called filming.[3]

Outside infra/superstructural dominance, capital anticipates a filmic *Gelassenheit*, in which a dehiscence of reason releases being from the sublime movement of the future. Concealed in a postmodern inundation of images, transcendental reflection is shattered in the felling of narrow, rational spacings. There are no longer any landmarks or particular points of reference. What "lingers" is what shines in neither an absolute nor a perspectival sense, invariably exceeding dialectic essence-appearance distinctions. Revealing the ruptured "existence of things" as interminable covering/discovering of a new veil, capital breaks the vanity of essences, appearances, and things themselves. Filming, disengaged from the rigorous reductions of *logos*, begins to free imagination for capital, a new "coming-toward" in which the felling of being does not stop with the subversion of pure epistemology but continues to disrupt the certainties of a theory-practice dialectic, particularly the parodic use of hermeneutics and metaphysics by political theorists.

It is important to see that this filmic excess and dehiscence of reason pertains to the matter (*die Sache*) of thinking (*Denken*). But much more precision is needed as to the question of thinking in the domain of filming. This question is always already part of a filmic unbinding of imagination from the narrow operations of an epistemology drawn of noumenal-phenomenal essences. Thinking, therefore, consists in challenging imagination to make a judgment regarding its freedom.[4] Kant articulates this possibility in relation to the "free play" of imagination in a transcendental-teleological manner. He does not discern, however, imagination's disruptive connection to the abyss of reason or capital. Nor does he demand that imagination review its abrupt *disparition*, its free felling and roaming. In a post-Kantian turn, imagination flows silently into the heterogeneous spheres of capital, whose spacings show no ontological presence.

Now that capital films rationality, judgment, revealed in imagination's turn from being-in-reason, must be carefully explored. *The Critique of Judgment* grants a reflective transformation of judgment that proceeds from a determinate disposition to an indeterminate, aesthetic reflection. One could argue that Kant's work converges with a dissociative reading of reflection, whose traces filming advances into postmodern modalities of thought (*Denken*). Necessarily, Kant professes a reflective process with a comprehensive teleology, albeit without the ontological certainty of absolute knowledge. Judgment operative in filming, however, cannot be bound to finality, not even the finality without purpose. In responding to the velocity of reason, imagination calls into question a bifurcated criterion of understanding. Consequently, it springs forth as a "movement of the mind," a sublime prolepsis of filming—capital. In a surprising passage, Kant briefly depicts a general sense of metaphysics' dehiscence:

> The mind feels itself raised in its own judgment . . . and abandoning itself to imagination and reason,—which, although placed in combination with imagination without any definite purpose, merely extends it,—yet it finds the whole power of imagination inadequate to its ideas. (*CJ*, 113)

While the Kantian operation exposes imagination in terms of infinite matter itself, filming unveils imagination in the wake of capital's futural *Geist—Gelassenheit*.[5] Is Heidegger's "higher acting" of *Gelassenheit* operative in filming's prolepsis?[6] In light of the sublime seizure of imagination by capital, is the designation "higher acting" still appropriate? A glance at capital's genealogy illuminates filming as an "event of the head." It is therefore not unusual to speak of capital (*caput*, "head") in terms of the futural flux of reason. Capital is not regarded as a master concept dominating the relation of forces; it stands ahead of "events" only in the sense that it is a "coming-toward," a proleptic mode of thought. A moving texture which cannot be captured or reduced to an unequivocal concept, capital "consists" of diffuse scenes of filming without a theory gripped within practical reflections.[7] If "higher acting" is complicitous with an overturning of the rigid interests of a theory/practice hermeneutic, it accords with the effacement of a normative dominance of images.

Marx fails to highlight the possibilities of imaginal dehiscence, in that his reflections on capital are entirely governed by a "repressive hypothesis," that is, by the idea that capital is essentially deleterious so long as it cannot be unfastened from the production of commodities. The very notion of commodity production is burdened by the theoretical and practical limitations of a narrowly framed dialectic which confines imagination to the teleology of essence-appearance distinctions and translates this confinement into a historic critique of capitalism. Imagination's incarceration in the logocentric region of universals does not even become an issue. In relation to filming, however, capital dissipates negative and positive socioeconomic mediations, so that the roots of history are not consonant with the Feuerbachian milieu of "species-being" (*Gattungswesen*). Instead, capital confers a *Gelassenheit* on *Geist*, freeing spirit of *Begriff* with its imposed historical power for a time that is to come (*Zukunft*). In brief, capital guides the "movement" of spirit, now withdrawn from the interest accommodations of a hermeneutic deep structure, into the disjunctive, nonnecessary terrain of

Gelassenheit, which obstructs the formation of another metaphysical network with a political ideology. As dynamic interplay of *Geist* and *Gelassenheit*, capital, always already ahead of metaphysical constructions of harmony or identity, precludes infra-superstructural analyses determined by a pre-decided teleology of meaning. In pursuit of this question, especially with regard to the modalities of capital as *Geist* and *Gelassenheit*, I want to consider briefly the concept of the beautiful-in-nature (*das Naturschöne*).

The beautiful-in-nature does not reveal nature, but rather what *tarries* when nature withdraws: the abyss of metaphysics in which the dialectic presence of consciousness fades. Aligned to what Adorno calls "second reflection," the beautiful-in-nature, which is not attached to an immediacy of images or imaging, steers toward a filmic judgment on "first nature," prior to nature's technological annexation. The beautiful, then, evokes a filmic eruption of appearances (*Erscheinungen*), or apparition, in which *spirit* opens "itself" to filmic "com-posure" (*Gelassenheit*). Granting non-identity to the inexpressible language of nature, the beautiful sways into a phenomenal explosion of objectivity without persisting in negativity. "As in music, the beautiful in nature is like a spark flashing momentarily and disappearing as soon as one tries to get hold of it" (*AT*, 107). And yet, against a negative dialectic, spirit's post-aesthetic beginning shows signs of a *promesse sans presence*.[8]

In so radical a spacing as capital, filming exceeds mimetic theory in relation to the beautiful-in-nature. Since capital, as social origin of alienation, is neither affirmed nor denied, *mimesis* is no longer a feasible aesthetic position. While transcending the production process of capital, filming renders (but does not *pass*) judgment on the contemporary scene. And yet, with regard to the beautiful-in-nature, capital marks the post-aesthetic site of spirit, whose com-posure indicates a countermetaphysical promise. The principle of exchange henceforth does not succumb to an Adornoian anathema, but becomes part of a nonidentical play of "forces" through which spirit is announced not as a "cipher of reconciliation" but as a filmic thwarting of presence. Viewing the com-posure of capital from the perspective of the beautiful-in-nature, is it possible that spirit is engaged in a commodified frame of thought? Does its metaphysically ephemeral "nature" merely exemplify a prosaic aesthetic movement of counter-history?

Briefly stated, *Gelassenheit* challenges the radical nihilism correlative with the end of metaphysics. It resists experimenting anew with metaphysical principles and declines to institute a new identity. While announcing imagination-in-transition, a thinking disinclined to make univocal judgments, *Gelassenheit* takes a different turn than that of critique. Its filmic vigilance heightens and intensifies the "free play" of judgment, releasing capital from a teleological alliance of dialectics and subversion. The beautiful-in-nature serves to guide imagination through the filmic apparition of images without confining imagination to the narrow spacings of the principle of sufficient reason. One might say that the beautiful-in-nature emerges as a promise without finality, com-posure's "own" promise of reason. A film of truth illuminates the spirit of this promise, which dwells in the fading image of beauty de-lighting in a Dionysian abyss of memory. The apparition tarries in a sublime play of collisions between the modalities of com-posure, spirit, and prolepsis. This play marks the groundlessness of metaphysics, the abyss (*buthos*) in thought, a philosophical apparition. Hence, what comes to mind in a filmic movement of capital is not the ground of being but the temporal abyss reflected in the shattered mirror of images, now transposed into the salient eye of a displaced imagination.

Without the metaphysical bedrock of the will, the filmic modalities of com-posure and spirit, which are not self-positing categories of a new system of reason, emerge as fissures of capital receding from a purely aesthetic-epistemic presence of images. *Gelassenheit* shows that filming not only disrupts imaging but also marks a decisive turn to a dehiscence of metaphysics that radically displaces imagination. Indeed, the "free play" of capital makes it more suitable to speak of filming rather than imagination per se. The name "filming" does not replicate the transcendental moorings of *Einbildungskraft*. Instead, it grants *Einbildung* its power (*Kraft*) by means of a non-teleo-imaginal movement of spirit.

Filming thinks capital as *first nature*, exceeding appearance and essence, absence and presence. An "apparition of images" links capital to the promise of "a second reflection," spirit's "postmodern" alliance with com-posure. Thinking the "apparition of images" in terms of capital is not only reflection *by* filming but also *of* filming.[9]

Posed in these terms, imagination's new domain begins with *Gelassenheit*'s nearness to capital, freeing spirit from the power of will. The eccentricity of such a shift to capital raises the question of the very movement of filming. What is here being moved? What is actually shown by imagination's dehiscence? Precisely what is spirit granted by *Gelassenheit*? And what awakens spirit to capital's de-limiting metaphysical implications?

Always already a formless "content" or apparition, capital signals the spirit of a time to come. Without arising in and of itself in the form of *natura naturans* or *natura naturata*, it reveals the power of "first nature," the discursive scene of *das Naturschöne*. Discourse serves as a clue to this "mysterious" terrain. For the beautiful-in-nature exists only in the inexpressible language of capital, whose spirit is not a *Zeitgeist* of postmodernism (since this epoch is far from a constellation of time and spirit) but a desire for a time without another absolute or "*transcendens* pure and simple." Discourse then awaits the arrival of the beautiful-in-nature in a "free filmic *Spielraum*" of spirit: "spacings of waiting," anticipating the com-posure of capital, more precisely "the new, the not-yet, the possible" (*AT*, 109). Accordingly, filming marks the decisive turn of imagination from the logocentric power of the will to a radical dispersion of spirit into capital.

As imagination breaks out of narrow epistemic, moral, and teleologic spacings, filming exposes capital to a discourse of power whose site opens a com-posure of spirit. This unique modality of filming lets capital be, and reveals a sublime movement in relation to a dawning of spirit (*Zukunft-schöne*). With regard to the filmic fissures of capital, what precisely is the character of "dawning" in its non-originary, futural appearance of filming? Instead of linking beauty to morality, filming displaces the transcendental determination of a judgment of taste by projecting the beautiful as a matter of capital's dawning, a matter of the filmic movement of the sublime. In this dawning, capital is always already what Kant calls the sublime, without the latter's constraint of a subjective finality. Hence, the sublime arises along with filming as an indeterminate order of capital beyond the abyss of the postmodern scene. This is not to say that the beautiful (dawning) and the sublime (capital) simply constitute a harmony within filming, but rather that they emerge as dissonant moments within *Gelassenheit*, and transpose the "first nature" of natural beauty to a "second reflection" of spirit. In turn, *Gelassenheit*, which cannot be read as epistemic, moral, or aesthetic identity, reveals spirit's dissonant language, and expunges the identity of noumenon and phenomenon so that only one "thing" appears—the apparition of images. Linked to apparition, spirit is not a new ideal of imagination. There are no more ideals in the open terrain of filming; only friction, collision, and dissonance belong to the filmic beauty of spirit's dawning in capital.

FILMING: DAWNING OF CAPITAL

Beyond appearance and essence, capital is seen as a "postmodern" roaming of filming, an evanescent, ruptured movement of spirit without originary unity or purpose, invariably disrupting the smooth surface of the dialectic as well as the ontologic interplay of presence and absence. Breaking out of its former metaphysical appearance, capital emerges as apparition, a sublime epistemic explosion of discontinuous images that shatters any ideological critique of capital. Withdrawn from historic teleology with its political vestiges of representation, capital exceeds concepts of profit or labor as revealed in conventional hermeneutic readings, and undergoes a radical transformation. The metaphysical idea of capital is inadequate for clarifying the filmic economy of the sublime. Precisely because it is not regarded as source and goal of production, capital is no longer solely aligned to the commodity structure of production. The question of capital explored in this text does not bind filming to capitalism. The evanescence of images, which filming signifies by its very com-posure, dissipates any notion of a common ground such as capitalism. It is, therefore, erroneous to conclude that the dehiscence of metaphysics, which filming displays, secures capital as a phenomenon within the territorialized functions and interests of a capitalist mode of production. While capital emerges from the filmic explosion of appearances, disrupting both identity and difference of the sensible and supersensible, spirit, in letting imagination be, awakens ever again the sublime art of apparition.

The difficulty that may arise in regarding capital as "art of apparition," withdrawn from metaphysics in general and the essence of technology in particular, will remain so long as capital is seen from the historic conditions of commodity production. Without filming, capital is confined to critical ideologies with a dogmatically secured discourse. Filming, however, frees capital from the historical script of presence and proceeds toward sublime apparition. In contrast to Kant's feeling of the sublime, neither nature nor teleology, neither morality nor critique belong to the spontaneous, discontinuous, indeed, *nonimaginal* movement of imagination. Now free to judge, imagination, displaced by capital, traces the explosion of appearances to the end of metaphysics and the beginning of a discursive com-posure of spirit.

Let me attend more closely to the question of capital within the filmic withdrawal from presence. In the course of imagination's departure from transcendental, epistemic, and technical enframing, capital, regarded as mirroring the power of filming, provides a "reflective" opening for imagination, one that ephemeralizes the relation of the noumenal and the phenomenal. This epistemic indeterminateness indicates filmic evanescence. Without positing appearances, a flux of images moves from one play of forces to another, so as then to vanish in the apparition of capital. There are no negations or positions, no identities or differences as these may be discerned in dialectical reflection. Instead, what is evident in this filmic interplay of apparition, in which fleeting images fade from their transcendental origin, is a dawning of spirit in mirroring fissures that expose the ends of substance and the felling of subjectivity. Nothing remains, nothing appears. Yet, images are seen scattering from one frame of reference to another in the explosive mirroring of capital. Spirit's new shining does not come from the displaced subject of the camera. Having no origins, aims or goals, it is *Lichtung*, reflecting the broken mirror of imagination. In a play of apparition, capital leads to a new site of spirit, signifying the uprooted power of imagination (*Einbildungskraft*). Invariably linked to filming, this power tears capital from capitalism and other metaphysical ventures in order to grant spirit an undefiled (*lautere*) discourse.[19]

The apparition of images qua apparition and the violent fissures of reason amid the inevitable silence of filming expose capital's ironic tensions of discourse. How does filming relate to capital's sublime discourse? Capital, for one, is uniquely diverse. It permeates the sundry modalities of filming, in particular, the technical strategies of power. Indeed, imagination's unleashing of the forces of images without epistemic-transcendental violence extends to technical *Ereignis*. The enframing limitations of technology, however, are delimited by filming insofar as capital as constellation of *Geist/Gelassenheit* is no longer determined by capitalist interests. On the contrary, these interests dissipate in capital's advancement toward the beauty of dawning. Dawning disrupts technology's power of enframing by introducing a discursive disposition in which the power of capital is revealed as "free spirit" of judgment. By virtue of its elective affinity with dawning, discourse attenuates the dialectic opposition within technology. While the current technological relationship with nature is entirely displaced, discourse confronts a striking gap: a world without nature, an epoch without *Geist*, indefinite unmediateness of capital, filmic dissonance of reason's com-posure. Discourse exceeds the polarity of subject and object, and is no longer the voice of *logos*, which today accommodates the communicative orientations of electronic technology. Refusing to be locked into moral or historical judgments which have constituted the presence of the subject, discourse is not concerned with ideological matters.[11] And yet, filming is empty without a discourse whose concerns belong to spirit's new dawn.

THE STRAYING OF CAPITAL

At this point we must take a closer look at capital in its radical "apparitional" exposure of spirit. Capital is a nonidentical "event" of filming, the "shattered instant" (*zerbrochene Augenblick*—the *kairos*) of imagination's mood (*Befindlichkeit*), the postmodern erosion of dialectical anchoring. Between the "transparency" of com-posure and the "white opacity" of spirit, capital is "the fortuitously opaque flash" of filming.[12] In its explosive *kinesis*, it strays from the immediacy of images to the displaced domain of shadowing. It is futile to see filming as a return to presence of objects or images, when it traces imagination's withdrawal from transcendental centering to an opening of *Geist*, in which capital displays its continuous adumbration of "decapitated" images. Apparition dissolves the electronic presence of images and the quotidian nature of its weightless communication. The fading of appearances in capital marks a decisive turn for thinking (*Denken*), wherein capital's filmic power (*Kunstkraft*) ex-plodes the phenomenal-noumenal textuality. "The shattered instant" engages thinking in a *glissement* of ontology, so as to reveal a filming invariably without epistemic constraints, even as images break away from what is being imaged. Still, what is mirrored is not the smooth surface of communication, or

Baudrillard's "nonreflecting surface." Indeed, capital is not surface at all but "a play of forces" dismantling imagination's conventional identity. If filming were merely a matter of elegantly inverting representation, it would bring about an ecstatic metaphysics of surface. It is crucial, therefore, not to render filming in its sublime movement of capital as a "thin" recentering of presence that would simply "reconstitute" a commodity aesthetics of the "pure screen." In these matters, filming is much more attentive to apparition and discontinuity, ideas introduced by Adorno and Foucault, than to Baudrillard's fruitful, fascinating metaphysical account of "simulations."

Our analysis shows clearly that filming tends toward an opening whose site reflects the untimely com-posure of capital colliding with spirit. Freed from metaphysical moorings, including the commodified aesthetics of technology, capital participates in a felling of capitalist closure, exposing imagistic fissures without the ideological tool of emancipation. Without raising reflection to higher positions, capital lets judging (*Ur-teil*) be. Straying from waves of images to instants of apparition, capital yields a filmic dispersal of spirit without the alliance of dialectic and hermeneutic explanations of the history of thought. As it strays from the "pure screen" of the Hollywood tyranny of images, and roams beyond a postmodern image-system, capital is more than a cursory glance at the ecstatic obscenity of commodified images.[13] Disengaged from mirroring a particular cultural space or *Zeitgeist*, it sketches time as a sublime straying from presence *and* simulation, in turn pointing away from the metaphysical signal of *Geist* to a disseminal constellation of *Geist* and *Gelassenheit*. Capital's sublime play of dehiscence erases the metaphysical urge to provide imagination the security (*Sicherheit*) of an absolute spirit conceived to be superior to nature. Straying from the power of presence, capital is not secured by the presence of any power. Power *is* capital, at most a sublime fading of spirit into sigetic homelessness. The filmic erosion of a "safe place" exposes the difference between spirit and imagination differently than what is presented in the *Critique of Judgment*. There is no awakening of a feeling of the supersensible in filming. Imagination encounters its limits from its "free play" *within* digression. Spirit is engaged in that very play, serving to enhance imagination's disruption without demanding conformity to the interest-accommodations of totality. Hence, the sublime becomes more deeply sublime in spirit's newly granted com-posure of filming, and projects a new site for capital at an unknown, luminous distance from ground.

8

◆

Surflectants—Strife of Filmic Surfaces

What is most notable in apparition is that images fade in conjunction with the withdrawal of essence-appearance discerned initially in Nietzsche's genealogy. Still, the slippage of objects grants surfaces of films in contrasting and shifting modes. What persists in view of the collapse of the thing is the film. A diffusion of film surfaces sets in motion a distinctive cascade of capital. Surface forces of capital film the precipitously slanting metaphysical paths of reason. Filming's eccentricity yields a surface power that consists of *surflectants* (sur[face] [re]flect[ive] a[ge]nts), which emerge from a disruption of presence. Surflectants exceed reflections in the "face" or *speculum* of the other, and manifest an a-specificity in a mode of judging that effaces the universal while dispersing the particular. With regard to surflectants, filming names a new literature of *Ur-teil*.

More pointedly, one may consider surflectants "reflective agents" of filming that linger on the surface of capital, projecting, undesignedly, *Gelassenheit's* "higher play" between spirit and imagination. In general, surflectants are the surface energies of films, discontinuous forms of displaced transcendental-empirical objects. By no means empty nihilistic surfaces of postmodernity, surflectants exceed Baudrillard's obscenity of communicative ecstasy, since they are not linked to capitalism's vertigo or the delirium of its production process. As trans-cultural coatings of metaphysical dehiscence, surflectants are free to move within the epistemic opening of imagination without losing their configuration of power, their concentration of films within capital.

What precisely are these surflectants? At first, they seem to arise as surface forces of films, displacing appearances and the things themselves. Reflective fissures of images continually undergoing metaphysical deactivation, they may also be described as filmic agents of capital whose sublime power of apparition effaces the bedrock of essentiality. As such they account for the felling, cascading, or filming of presence. Destabilizing objects, surflectants also attend to what capital yields in the cascading process of apparition. As surface forces of capital, they withdraw from narrow logocentric spacings within the infra- and super-structural regions of social ontology. In turn, they cannot be regarded as ethical or political agents in the service of postmodernity. Here the name "agent(s)" is merely rendered as "waves of surfaces" exerting power on the filmic flow of capital, without dominating particular surface-energies or capital in its configurations.

The power in capital is notably a "free play" of surflectants, or striking instants which point beyond the postmodern curve of filming. Capital is not an aggregate of surflectants, but rather dehiscent spacings in which surflectants play out their withdrawal from objects and images of the photologocentric terrain. Capital, the power that makes surface forces of films possible without falling into reflective nihilism, is spirit cascading outside a dialectic of subject and object, non-teleologically aligned to the beautiful-in-the-future. Its non-necessitarian endeavor is to prevent a reconstruction of essencing which would stifle the elegant power of capital's filmic cascade and obstruct imagination's itinerary toward filmic freedom. Capital withdraws from imaginal alliances with rationality or any essencing. Spirit's disengagement may also be taken as capital's apparition, paving the way for a "spiriting," an *oratio* of judging that is not anti-epistemic. Within filmic withdrawal, spirit explodes the narrow spacings of reason without doing violence to thinking (*Denken*). In turn, filming brings metaphysics to an end, opening imagination toward the kinetic site of capital, the silence of reason's com-posure. A new mood (*Befindlichkeit*) sets in motion the sublime collision of surflectants, a mood of filmic roaming outside the sphere of essencing. Moving in an uprooted space of imagination, filming radically disrupts the tendency of socio-political judgments to maintain an ideological dominance in a world of social technology. The non-teleologic movement of surflectants marks the conditions for the possibility of a new critique of capitalism, on the view of a post-aesthetic of filming, in accordance with the very apparition of capital.

Capital: Filmic Art of Swaying ('Schwanken')

A post-aesthetic is here bound up with a filmic art of swaying (*Schwanken*) from an aesthetic of "second reflection" to imagination's "own" site, a "free play" of judging, opening spirit to the sublime itinerary of filming. In filmic operations, a post-aesthetic points to imagination-in-transition, a swaying in which capital sets itself in motion, exceeding the enframing challenge of technology. Although intertwined, art and capital are not the same. Capital proceeds from the filmic fissures of images to an apparition in which art reveals surflectants. Arguably, art (*Kunst*) is what capital does (*können*) and what is anticipated in capital's filmic swaying. As "free play of thought," art turns capital from commodified aesthetic imagery and grants imagination the freedom to judge without the taint of essencing. Art emerges as a "principle" foreign to the logocentric mode of reflection. Indeed, an inter-weaving of filming, capital, and surflectants in respect of art indicates that these are not *principia domestica* of philosophy per se, but at the most *lemmata*, auxiliary thoughts to *principia peregrina*, that is, to foreign "prin-ciples" of thinking. This does not make thinking conducive to poetry. On the contrary, it opens thinking to a post-aesthetic of filming. Such a post-aesthetic is neither purely scientific nor poetic. Nor is it something vague, as might be thought if one were to invite art as *principium peregrinum* to play an "intermediary" role. But here art does not play such a role. While mediation is dialectically out of control, art is very methodical in its undoing of metaphysics' narrow channeling, and demands that capital be taken off the modernist and postmodernist stage so that surflectants as artistic dis-positions may grant ever more opening to a nonhierarchical constellation of spirit and imagination. These post-imaginal artistic forces, which animate capital in withdrawing from a commodity aesthetic, also free art *from* aesthetics itself *for* "imagination's rapidly passing play."[1] In the wake of apparition, surflectants point to dis-positional modes of capital whose filmic undoing of aesthetics opens into an immense field of post-aesthetic possibil-ities. Without vanishing in the sublime movement of capital, art withdraws from aesthetics and, more importantly, from its historico-transcendental origins. This double withdrawal makes possible an unforeseeably new spirit, a filming whose literature of capital sways from imaginal free play to the anti-art of a fractured ground of judging (*Ur-teil*).

Inevitably, art, art work, and artist coalesce in the filmic agitation of capital. Transformed into modes of withdrawal, these modalities drift unen-cumbered along capital's discontinuous flux of surflectants. In search of spirit, imagination sheds its metaphysical skin and sets in motion spaces of com-posure as filming softly focuses on capital breaking out of the seductive illusions of a commodity world. The unsettling *kinesis* of surflectants, abruptly departing from postmodern scenes, reveals the end of technology's domination and a dawning of capital, whose "theory" cannot restore the dialectic to subjectivity by constructing more ethical and political alterna-tives. In light of imagination's drifting and straying, radically felling the once familiar subject with desires of narrow spacings, one wonders whether there is a mode of thought that does not wane and fade? Does the filmic art of swaying in its ironic luminosity signify anything but capital outside a phenomenal-noumenal world? Is this filmic play of withdrawal merely a *Gedankenspiel*, or has thinking never been more seriously at play than in a filmic withdrawal from the world of things? Is it even possible to withdraw from the immediacy of world-images and its praxeological interests? These questions can only be answered in accordance with the possibility of filming's disjunctive, non-necessary modes of judgment. Withdrawal must, therefore, be conceived of differently from domesticated criticisms and hermeneutic delimitations of philosophy as critique. More than a critique of judgment, which has obtained primarily a critique of imagination, there is a decisive need for a filmic judgment on critique itself. Accordingly, filming serves to free judgment for a "critique" of critique, without being haunted by a historical presence of capital.

Capital's "counter-images" withdraw from the grip of presence, as surflectants or films of spirit grant ever more openness to imagination in its post-imaginal swaying. Drifting from essentiality, filming may now concentrate its economy of surflectants on capital's most dehiscent art mode—dis-course. As narrative of the sublime, dis-course (*discurrere*, Lat., "to run about") is not only the idiom of capital but also the anticipatory trace of spirit. Hence, discourse does not stand outside or above surflectants but flows within the filmic execution of surflections. Surflection is here the name for a free and open mode of judging in imagination, replete with capital's most diverse operational dis-positions. Discursive surflectants, therefore, unveil what exceeds the unique narratives of films as well as the diegetic movements of speech and writing in general. More importantly, as capital's own narrative, dis-course moves all of the filmic operations toward the most transgressive site of filming, where spirit collides with *Gelassenheit*. This dis-cursive clearing of capital does not surpass filming. On the contrary, dis-course cannot be without filming, without the coating and felling of metaphysical investments. Perhaps dis-course is the matter (*die Sache*) of filming without the matter of reflection *itself*. Or, more precisely, dis-course is correlative with com-posure, capital's sublime speaking of filming's serene surflections.[2] Accordingly, dis-course echoes the baffling economy of capital placed "in the middle" of judgment's fracture (*Ur-teil*). Swaying from essentiality of apparition, it supplements a post-aesthetic of filming and ends a mimetologic narrative of art.

CAPITAL—POWER ('AUCTORITAS') WITHOUT SUBJECT

Spirit's advance to a new site of authority,[3] the surflections of capital, marks a filmic slippage of essence-appearance by virtue of which judgment is no longer bound to an imaginal play of presence and absence. The authority that fades into capital is indeed apparitional. Authority is here brought to light as power in filming, a disposition of imagination without being. So constituted, authority does not find guidance in moral and political passions. The subject ceases to have a position. This does not mean, however, that capital stages an anonymous totalitarian power which ensnares the filmic forces of the present age. The open concept of capital in light of filming's authority is conceived ostensibly as spirit's freedom from rigid norms and hierarchies.

Correlatively, *auctoritas* is not consonant with anarchy. Indeed, capital does not narrow its circle of movements to a reckless region of empty tremorings. In a postmodern sense, capital is authority (*Ansehen*) of a time to come, where spirit sees what cannot be seen yet. The abstract power of capital does not dis-appear into late-capitalist nihilism simply because it serves no dialectical *telos*. Implicit in a modality of authority that is no longer a political category is a unique mode of seeing, *Gelassenheit's* dissonant force in a post-marxian itinerary of filming.

Authority's passage into imagination's non-essential, non-phenomenal movement of time enhances spirit's freedom by means of the sublime spacings of capital that transgress the simulations of images. Authority (*Ansehen*) is, therefore, free from authority, from history in a postmodern exposure of capital through filming. Anew, while capital moves without being present, it is more powerful than any previous authority and more authorial than any institution. Without a subject it exceeds itself and shatters all interpretations of itself. Indeed, it does not exist in itself, but moves only within imagination's free opening, where spirit shows com-posure and capital may transpose "everything." Capital's authority comes from spirit's turn to *Gelassenheit*, a turn or *Kehre* that extends the terrain of surflectants from the beauty of nature to what may become beautiful-in-the-future. The film of ambiguity in capital's authority deflects from falling into political exhaustion, which would invariably delegate power to a subject.

Authority in capital does not claim the power of an individual, stretched, as it were, along and between forces and relations of production. Instead, an authorial movement in the hands of "imagination" will provide an avenue of entry into capital's subversion of capitalism and communism. Eliding authoritarian interests, surflectants transpose capital into a kinetic work of spirit, whose play of withdrawal dissipates the hegemonic presence of subject. In turn, capital is not a representation of power but a falling of power from reason to imagination, that is, from essencing to filming. This filmic fall indicates that power is precisely what cannot be represented, what cannot be secured or grounded in ideological, technical, or commodified comforts of presence. Indeed, capital is power (*auctoritas*) above infra-superstructural dimensions, exceeding its historic-metaphysical appearance and its old mimetic essence. Inevitably, capital is filming's *Blicksprung*: a unique mode of judging in which "things" leap into apparition without exposing themselves to representation.

As imagination breaks out of the anchoring terrain of teleology, its *auctoritas*, which shines forth as capital, creates a "sigetic" mode of spirit linked to, yet not limited by, postmodernity.[4] Spirit, supplementing writing, passes through subversive spacings of postmodernism. Advancing beyond images toward the uncanny "epistemic" site of apparition, spirit's unsettling authority (*Ansehen*) awakens judgment without seeking a purpose in filming. Paradoxically, spirit's power of opening into capital derives from the sublime withdrawal of the principle of sufficient reason. In turn, filming invariably concerns capital as a post-aesthetic "counterprinciple" of spirit, freeing imagination from the pale cast of its transcendental services and, more importantly, from its production of images. What flows out of this stream of withdrawal (*Abkehr*) from the order of ground is a power of abstraction whose spirit throws off a preordained sequence of forms, and grants surflectants the silent dis-course of *Gelassenheit*, a nonoriginary authority.[5] In this sense, spirit "acts" on various surface levels of power in a process of felling which leaves no things to themselves. Without sedimenting films of events, filming beyond a postmodern "art" of judgment unleashes representation from the prosaic lull of rationality, while capital drifts and strays as filmic engagement of *Geist/Gelassenheit*. Capital, radiating its sheen upon surflectants whose incomparable forces film the "end of images," sets in motion an authorial strife of spirit which reveals an unforeseeably new art, filming's post-aesthetic.

9

◆

Filming—A Postmodern Mode of Judgment

Writing, which signifies "the most formidable difference" (*OG*, 56), does not submit to a phenomenological sense of seeing, yet it rests upon a linguistic framework with a unique philosophical name. Filming, however, is neither bound to submit to sight, since capital as apparition cannot really be seen, nor is it bound to submit to a unique philosophical naming (such as *differance*), since it is impervious to a metaphysical genealogy. What, then, is the relation between a "postmodern" mode of thought such as filming and deconstruction? If filming concerns a *glissement* of essentialist thinking, if it probes into a fading of the dialectic, particularly the dialectic of noumenon and phenomenon, of essence and appearance, is it not closely related to the deconstructive enterprise, notably Derrida's disseminative view of writing?

Since this is not the place for a detailed inquiry into this question, I merely want to outline some distinctions and interrelations among filming and writing. Writing is an "indefinite pivoting," a mode of thought which does not mediate, master, sublate, or dialecticize. Deconstructive thinking withdraws from the "dialectic happiness" of *Aufhebung* and inscribes the memory of thought in the interval of contradiction and non-contradiction. The text grants an uncanny play of disruption, a tearing of the hermeneutic veil, a bursting apart of reflection. Breaking out of its academic spacings, deconstruction, however, is merely the beginning of a dehiscence of reflection. Postmodern thinking extends the operation of dissemination more radically as it films the sublime contours of judgment at this century's end. What Derrida says of dissemination can be said more specifically of the postmodern mood: "It outwits and undoes all ontologies, all philosophemes, all manner of dialectics" (*D*, 215). The implacable difference, however, between writing and filming is that while writing envelops dialectics, turns it over, and plays it out in a game of nonpenetration (*D*, 215), so as to bring to light the conditions for the possibility of an *entre*, a speleology of metaphysics, filming dissipates the principle of ground and the very conditions for the possibility of this principle upon which dialectic is constituted. Even in its withdrawal from dialectic, deconstruction cannot break out of the process of critique. So long as its mirror of reflection is unbreakable, it merely deflects from metaphysics. Filming, on the other hand, is the very shattering of this mirror,[1] an "aesthetic" impaling of the taint of *mimesis* from which philosophy surfaces as a ghost ship of deconstruction's last voyage. Far from the commanding script of a metaphysical past, filmic thought exceeds the "interval," "which is cannily interposed between [the] two silences" of reading and writing (*D*, 223), that deconstructive trace which cuts itself off from the signified. Even the general text is erased as a new dynamics of power comes on the scene, a power which does not extend the hermeneutic desire of interpretation into a terrain of grafting one form of writing onto another. Although Derrida claims that writing has no essence or value of its own, its play of simulacrum takes place within the propaedeutic configurations of philosophy. Indeed, writing is a *propaideuein*, a "preparing for" or "teaching" of conditions prior to the dialectic script of reason. Derrida's "arche-writing" is precisely what Gasche calls "a construct, aimed at resolving the philosophical problem of the very possibility [of metaphysics]" (*TM*, 274).

Deconstruction, then, emerges as the condition for new possibilities of reflection, originally grounded in *arche*. It uncovers possibilities of truth disclosed "between" the dismantling of philosophy as metaphysics and a deconstructive self-opening of philosophy as spacing. Hence, writing is filming's most powerful challenge, as it grants postmodern avenues an entry into "slippage . . . spreading truth even into untruth, separating it from itself in a way that would once have been called separation *as such*, [into] the advent of crisis, a crisis of truth, of reason" (*S*, ix). While such disruptive play turns against the logocentric genealogy, reflection, albeit polysemic, lingers within a genealogy of differences as writing presumes to escape the dialectic. Filming now has a double task: first, to examine the felling of essencing in general; and second, to think the last shadow of essence, namely, deconstruction, a disseminative reflection of metaphysics' felling. Effacing presence also assumes the self-erasure of the minimal infrastructures of deconstruction. Still, it remains to be seen whether filming, in thinking capital differently, exceeds writing, or whether, along with a dehiscence of spirit, filming operates too much within and without deconstruction.

Similarly, one may also ask how far thinking imposes on the "fringe of irreducibility" (*Po*, 67)? Derrida himself indicates that it may be necessary to "redouble our prudence in reconsidering the problem of meaning and reference," and notes that "the outside can always become again an 'object' in the polarity subject/object" (*Po*, 67). How can filming avoid such danger and still exceed deconstruction's efforts to trace the limits of philosophy? Is filming's judgment of capital as apparition more radical than Derrida's deconstruction of the ethico-theoretical hierarchy of the dialectic? These questions can only be answered adequately if it can be shown that writing is merely a reflective incision that ruptures totalization. Undoubtedly, this is a task beyond the theme of this text. Nevertheless, Derrida's claim that deconstruction is no longer a philosophy of essence must be examined briefly in order to outline more clearly the distinctions between writing and filming. Derrida notes that "writing *has* no essence or value of its own, whether positive or negative. It plays within the simulacrum" (*D*, 105). From the perspective of filming, however, the deconstructive play within simulacrum is still originary, making the difference of appearance and essence possible. Proto-writing is not engaged in a radical effacement of simulacrum, so a "phenomenal *mimesis*," even without a signified, still mimes the dialectical method. Filming extrudes simulacrum from the possibility of "reflective" efficacy in projecting capital as a trace of spirit's apparition. As "pure" apparition, surflectants are dislodged from the technical relations of pure appearing, phenomena, noumena, what appears, mere appearances, and simulacra. Even, or especially, in its apparitional play, capital eviscerates the idea of simulacrum. In the domain of filming, spirit dispels any attempts to found capital as a concept so as not to repeat the presence of *eidos* within or without simulacrum. Playing within simulacrum, writing does not necessarily collapse dialectical relations. On the contrary, in such a play, the want of a signified is transposed into the "presence" of a disseminative nonpresence, a mere folding back upon the dialectical *eros*. Arguably, the seduction of presence is more powerful in writing's play within simulacrum than in the metaphysical drama of *mimesis*, assuming, of course, that pleasure is still linked to the spacings of writing. Derrida notes: "Memory always already needs signs in order to recall the nonpresent, with which it is necessarily in relation. The movement of dialectics bears witness to this" (*D*, 109).

While Derrida's philosophy insists that writing is not gripped in essence, it shows that writing is the condition for the possibility of essence. In its search for an entirely different text, deconstruction "re-marks" the dialectic, perhaps without a binary presence of *logos* but not without the general text of an originary system of relations. So, in the end, deconstruction accommodates a contemporary metaphysics of relations. Proto-writing touches the core of the problem of relations "between" presence and absence. Although Derrida does not identify proto-writing with origin as the *arche* of *prima philosophia*, the idea of origin lies in the metaphoricity of the relations between "beginning" and "becoming." Essence is no longer regarded as one grand metaphor, or as metaphysics' "old dream of symmetry,"[2] but as an infinite plurality of metaphors. This irreducible plurality of metaphors, however, merely displaces the history of being without disvaluing essence. Derrida radicalizes Hegel's emphasis on the metaphoric "interruption of the course of ideas" without indicating the end of the metaphoric. He writes: "Metaphor always carries its death within itself. And this death, surely, is also the death *of* philosophy" (*M*, 271). The genitive here is indeed double, as Derrida notes. While deconstruction belongs to the *genetivus subjectivus* end of a particular way of doing philosophy, notably with regard to the transcendental-horizonal method, filming addresses the *genetivus objectivus* end of philosophy, which "is no longer to be refound within philosophy" (*M*, 271). Deconstruction's attempt to withdraw from all teleology, even in the disseminative process of metaphor's self-effacement, cautiously ventures toward a new ground, *eine neue Bödenstandigkeit*, which brings to light the very principle upon which and from which it can be argued that there is no ground. Like the Stoic face of metaphoric consciousness, this new formless movement of thought reveals another philosophical possibility for the conditions of a dialectic.

Serving to posit no originary structures, filming radically questions "the beginning and end of philosophic" discourse, without disregarding the importance of exposing a concept of judgment no longer fastened to a self-reflexive relation of reason. Writing, as named by Derrida, does not explicitly thematize the question of difference in judgment (*Ur-teil*), particularly with regard to imagination's new itinerary.[3] Although Derrida's philosophy begins to crystallize a new turn in the movement of spirit, notably in *La Vérité en peinture*, it does not clarify the question of imagination's displacement in view of the strife of the primordial ground (*Ur*) and the particular dispersion (*Teil*) of judgment.

In these matters, Sallis' *Spacings—Of Reason and Imagination* may be more fruitful. He argues that the contemporary predicament of philosophy, that is to say, the crisis of reason, can only be expounded from the perspectives of a radical displacement of imagination. Accordingly, Sallis discerns an opening in judgment with regard to imagination's outbreaks of spacing. In some instances, his thinking prepares the way for a filmic dehiscence of metaphysics much more decisively than the uncertain territority opened by the texts of Heidegger or Derrida. Precisely at the point where imagination is set free, at the point where the power of judgment subjugates its "stock of images" (*S*, 156), at the site of a radical withdrawal from presence, he seems to align a subversive reading of the imaginal to a "final spacing of metaphysics," indeed, to an "excess of spirit" without *mimesis*.

While filming disengages Sallis' hesitation to "space" reason into epochal fields of "culture," it takes his idea of "spacings" to the hilt by revealing a mode of judging (*Ur-teil*) that is severed from and in excess of its former dialectic and of its mystic relations to originary and final spacings of metaphysics.

GENEAFILMIC TURN TO 'UR-TEIL'

I shall briefly highlight filming's unique connection to judgment. If judgment in general is made explicit as thinking the particular as contained under the universal, a "postmodern" mode of judgment may denote thinking without a metaphysical emphasis on the relation of the particular and the universal. Indeed, neither the particular nor the universal play a designative role in filming, only surflectants, or filmic dis-positions, which deflect from the principle of ground that no longer grounds reflection. A mirror of thought now mirrors itself without seeing itself. Are we merely advancing a pure theory of relativism? Where is thinking falling in its "geneafilmic" turn to "*Ur-teil*," filming's unique post-aesthetic "*Blicksprung*"?[4] What remains "outside" the dialectic and beyond Americanization, the current electronic perception of world? How can filming exceed even images of cinemas, which already signify a nonpresent presence? It is clear that images of films—whether they are produced in Hollywood, Munich, or Paris—are largely determined by a socio-mimetic impulse. *Mimesis* is still the core of filmmaking and, to be sure, of film theory. Filming, however, cannot be guided by a mimetic act. As it fades from the scene of things, even from the screen of images, filming appears without appearing while thinking the nonimaginal. A theory-practice erosion reveals a new constellation of thought: the apparition of capital and the com-posure of spirit (*Geist/ Gelassenheit*).

Once *phainesthai* is deontologized, filming "activates" judgment's disruption, severing its dis-course from received metaphysical formations whose determinate, logical, and aesthetic manifestations appear to have locked imagination into limited and limiting channels. In the wake of a felling of the dialectic relation of the particular and the universal, judgment, in spite of its *Verlegenheit* ("displacement"), must now discover its "new" matter of thought. Withdrawn from the table of the logical functions of categories and from the transcendental relation of imagination and reason, judgment is set adrift toward a new terrain: the dis-positional scene of filmic com-posure.

Accordingly, filming exposes the detour of judgment: judgment's *Kehre*, an *Abkehre* from representational images, from commodified, ideologized forces in general. Through filming, judgment breaks out of regulative and constitutive instances of reflection, emerging as imagination's power, the force of imagination's "postmodern" formation (*Einbildungskraft*). In this regard, judgment divides imagination as imaging the power of capital in apparition from a mere production faculty of images. It seems to demand of imagination a *phainesthai* of difference, a shining of its falling, dividing, differing (*teilen*), a receding from the power of *primal* metaphysical distractions (*Ur*). Now imagination asserts its connection to the paradoxical situation of judging the abyss, whose semblance reveals capital as apparition.

It must be recognized here that capital signifies powerful spacings of filming, with surflectants emerging amid the felling of theory and practice. As an epoch of thought "after" metaphysics (*Ur-teil*), capital eludes definition. Perhaps it is the mime of time without finality, *phainesthai* without being, without care but not without a filmic com-posure of spirit. As apparition, there is no appearance or proper showing of capital. So regarded, filming judges capital as a showing of power, not to be construed as will to power, nor even as a genealogical understanding of power according to Foucault's philosophy. Power (*auctoritas*) lets capital be. Here, *mimesis* fades as images vanish from the reflective screen of being into a postmodern frame of *Gelassenheit*, not in a mystic or poetic but in a filmic sense. Nothing, however, is really slipping away. Everything is there as it always has been, as it is and always will be. Filming's contribution is only that of a question: What about spirit in an epoch that lets capital be? Its demand on judgment is complex not because capital is perceived to be a scene that films well but because capital leaps ahead of its time in search of a spirit whose time is yet to be. Does *Gelassenheit* become *Verlassenheit*? Does com-posure turn into *destitution* in the wake of the apparition of capital, the felling of ground and meaning? Is com-posure of spirit the complete erasure of history, of substance, of foundation? Is filmic excision poverty of life and being, a universal destitution?

Only a strict adherence to the principle of ground would make it possible to incriminate some relation of *Gelassenheit* to *Verlassenheit*. From the dis-positions of filming, com-posure is neither negative nor positive, neither theoretical nor practical. A filmic withdrawal from ground may seem to awaken an idea of judgment that is empty and blind. Certainly, Kant thought that concepts without intuitions are unwarranted. Still, a "genea-filmic" judgment differs from a purely epistemic conception of thinking in an epoch when thought desires to be released from a certain economy of representation. Filming, therefore, exceeds the anthropological limit as it points to images that fade from subject in exposing capital. A *phainesthai* not peculiar to being is brought to light: the apparition of "something naturally beautiful." Yet, neither nature nor the image of nature is aligned to the beautiful-in-nature. This beauty belongs to a judgment, free of natural essence and appearance, as it steps out of the science of dialectic into filming's open but elusive epoch; whence a post-aesthetic that only apparition brings to view. What is naturally beautiful, then, is capital's apparition, of concern primarily to filming, whose unique exit from the mimetic order entails a dis-positional showing without a speculum of "something." The issue, then, is to acknowledge filming as com-posure (*Gelassenheit*) and not as *Aufhebung* of spirit.

While modern philosophy first clings always and only to consciousness, filming shows that judgment becomes "the matter" of spirit within a filmic falling of ground. Rendered as apparition, capital exposes a "new ground," spirit's imaginal opening, a dehiscence of judgment. In an epoch peculiar to a radical displacement of being, filming reveals the gap, the abyss, the cultural vacuum which follows from technology's ascent. While marking a new economy of imagination (*Einbildungskraft*), filming unbinds the metaphysical power of judgment (*Ur-teil*) from a photological identity of a primordial *before* (*Ur*) and a dispersive *after* (*Teil*), so as to be able to discern the post-aesthetic paradox of capital. It follows that filming does not presume to be *Uberwindung* ("overcoming") but *Verwindung* ("coming to terms") with *prima philosophia*, a fading and falling from the principle of western consciousness, *das Sein*. Neither inside nor outside of metaphysics, filming seems more like a metaphysical probing and judging. Having fallen from being's mimetic ground, filming is "carried away" (*entrückt*) toward a time yet to come, an open theatre whose screen is imageless. There, time is without ground, without being, without *Dasein*. It is judgment's new art, capital no longer conferring presence, no longer metaphysics, yet "metaphysical." The passage of judgment into filming marks a radical trembling for thought (*Denken*) as it swerves from the ontological course of *Ge-stell* to a filmic appearing of the nonimaginal.

Exergue: Fassbinder, Herzog, and 'Brightness Playing'

And lovely apparitions,—dim, at first,
Then radiant as the mind, arising bright . . .
From the embrace of beauty (whence the forms
Of which these are the phantoms) casts on them
The gathered rays which are reality—
Shall visit us, the progeny immortal
Of Painting, Sculpture, and rapt Poesy,
And arts, though unimagined, yet to be.

(Shelley, *Prometheus Unbound*)

FILM AND FILMING

Films break into the world and grant a view of being that is above and beyond the viewer's images. At times, a discursive modality bursts the imaginal filament of a film so that judgment can fill the filmic gap. Cutting deeply into images of the film, the gap tears the veil of representational illusion and exposes a decisively different reading of world from that of any particular film. The film films the gap of judgment (*Ur-teil*), a singular imaginal cut, a new way of seeing, a nonimaginal *phainesthai* derived in part from words and images of primary representation. The gap in the story of films begins with a rupture in representation. While representation does not vanish, it directs the constellation of image and discourse into a nonidentical milieu of coating, felling, and falling. From this ensues a radical dispersion of *Gegenstand*. The warp of images is wefted to a line no longer visible in filming. In turn, filming guides the imaginal to its fall, as apparition opens the scene for a different mode of thought between the *Ur* and *Teil* of judging. Indeed, the film is but a glancing moment of a "primordial segment" (*Ur-teil*) of judgment, which, while it grants a nondialectic layer of

105

reflection, cuts through the surface of technology's enframing. Judgment now ruptures the film of *logos* with its dialectic reflections of world.

The conventional structure of films corresponds to a dialectic mode of representing being, revealing a subject not so much looking at the world as looking *"out at* it" from the perspective of reason.[1] Whether it be Platonic, Kantian, or Hegelian, the dialectic appears as film of western culture, initially viewed through the eyes of *eidos*, and later conceived of from the perspectives of an egophantic reflection. *Logos*, a uniquely refined but highly problematic film of western thought, an extension of the dialectic film of the Socratic mind, an odd fancy indeed, draws a luminous veil before the eye of nature, coating being with moral substance while blemishing the beauty of the subject. As it throws a film of reason over becoming, the dialectic covers being with a sequential train of dim and hazy images mirroring reflection. Filmmaking today, especially the Hollywood film-ontology, typifies a common, infrastructural, ideological transformation of the coating peculiar to the dialectic insofar as world is shown from the perspectives of good and evil, a viewing always in binary dimensions. Even the so called "better films," which attempt to sublate moral oppositions with images of mediated identities, instead of creating "visions" merely produce videos. Consequently, these films fall into "visional exhaustion," a cruder and no doubt more comforting subjectivity than that of modern philoso-phy.[2]

Since imagination no longer lingers by the stagnant pool of logocentric confinement, a "geneafilmic" turn perforates the dialectic.[3] Films begin to manifest a cultural dehiscence of imagination, a breaking out of the transcendental walls of subjectivity. Imagination begins to judge. And philosophy's gift to humankind, the fading power of the dialectic, is *placed-on-view*. Despite common appropriations of the dialectic in filmmaking, imagination's open site of judgment exerts its influence culturally. Indebted in part to Heidegger's and Adorno's thinking, the new German cinema expressly attends to a disruptive opening of judgment, which perhaps has not been sufficiently articulated in philosophical discourse today. This direction challenges the Hollywood tyranny of images as well as the historical dominance of Athens' dialectic.

'FILMING IS ABOUT TO BEGIN . . .'

With regard to these matters, filming's flight from the order of ground invites discussion in such cinematic contexts as Werner Herzog's *The Mystery of Kaspar Hauser* and Rainer Werner Fassbinder's *Despair*. In both films, imagination trembles at the limit of its possibilities, eventually breaking free of the aesthetic embeddedness in an ethical or political ground. This postmodern flight from historical individuation seems at first to be antithetical to the film projects of Herzog and Fassbinder. But beyond a hermeneutic glance at these two films, one is not surprised to find that their work evokes a mode of judgment which opens the imaginal, linking it to apparition rather than imagination. What occurs is precisely a tearing up of representation, with images wandering freely from imagination as appearances fade into an abstraction of visual particularities in spite of the clarity of technical imagery which is, of course, merely subject to a concrete, historical perceiving. Reason is no longer filmed dialectically. This becomes evident in Kaspar Hauser's inability to ascertain the origin of the subject and in Hermann Hermann's spectatorial gaze at self-dissemination. Appearances and judgments rooted in appearances withdraw into a "sublime" terrain of apparition, where imagination is torn not only from reason's dominance but also, and more importantly, from its consequential "free play" of images. Filming is therefore viewed as the "look" of judgment, *der Blick des Urteils*, the *thea* of *phainesthai*. This "look" reveals judgment's fall from the order of the principle of ground, so that images capture imagination as it comes to its end in a different beginning.

Despair sets in as the set illuminates the disappearance of Hermann's identity. Lydia, his wife, appears merely as an effigy behind the glass of his idiosyncratic reflections. The *mimesis* falters even as the painter Ardalion attends to Lydia's desires to "ground" her dreams. There are no more characters in Herzog's and Fassbinder's films. All that lingers are instants of illumination with names to show the sublime action of *mimesis'* strife with itself. As viewers of a different mode of seeing, we are drawn into a movement of images whose power of discourse exceeds the representation of those particulars shown in such great detail. The irony of this filmic outbreak lies in desolate, naked, and apparitional images. And still, this very transparency, which leads the viewer from one detour of perception to another, opens a path for thinking which grants filming a new look at the very process of judgment, a *thea* telling the story of "our time" in its disruptive relation with representation. Withdrawn from the ontological ground of imagination, Herzog's images project a narrative in which judgment appears displaced in configurations of a new historical scene that cannot be seen, filmed, heard, or told. While only writing may seem to limit the unlimitedness of Herzog's desire for a radically different terrain, even the legal comfort of the written word vanishes in the filmic nonpresence of essence and appearances. The socio-cultural attempts to educate Kaspar Hauser and to bring him into the structural domain of civilization dissolve when faced with Herzog's powerful counter-image of a possible "first nature," a mimetic paradox, a *phainesthai* shining at the abyss of imagination.

Both Herzog and Fassbinder consider writing—which prompts thinking to name the matter of difference—to be metaphysical, primarily because writing is not in complicity with the sublime technology of imagery. Only a technology in its "mechanical reproduction" of representations can effectively confront the dominance of representation. If writing were aligned with the *thea* of technology's *aletheia*, it would be strikingly close to filming, especially since filming is not an activity of imaging but the sight of judgment (*der Blick des Urteils*). According to Herzog, difference is a matter of judgment, inasmuch as judgment is discord, *Zerissenheit*, the strife of *mimesis* possible on account of technology's presence as *Ge-stell.* Imagination's strife, its falling from subject, is the condition for the possibility of cinematic imagery. The disruptive "free play" of imagination continues with the camera's nearing, distancing, and straying of images. No more do the players on this filmic montaging know the significance of their play. Particular images may form a totality of appearances, yet this totality itself does not appear. The scene turns manifold appearances, which disappear into apparition.

Totality is still obtained in the image but not in imagination. Torn from the vertical structure of reason, totality hovers in fleeting moments, in instants of a radically new mode of judging. It no longer determines the process of judgment, but speaks in a filmic image, as in Fassbinder's *Journey into the Light*, when Hermann Hermann remarks: "Filming is about to begin . . ." as he reflects upon his homelessness. Imagination disseminates and speaks in *Despair*: "What if it's all a lie? We are making a film here, I am a film actor. I am coming out. Don't look at the camera . . . I am coming out."[4]

Judgment's glance at madness prevails throughout this film. Madness begins, it seems, when imagination ends in *mimesis*' strife with itself. There, Hermann Hermann forbodes a certain operation, a breaking out of representation, at least an attempt to end the dance with a counter-subject fading into illusory absence. The disintegration of his double identity, evidenced in the fatal fall of Felix, prompts representation into disarray. No conscience calls for retribution. An elegant swaying deflects the images from a "free play" of murder to the graceful rhythm of a "new enlightenment," the beginning of a journey into the light. While despair becomes a mere fall from hope in finality, filming grants no ground for hope. There is only capital without the economy of presence and absence. All the fantasies of capitalism have withdrawn into apparition. Hermann Hermann observes the end of a system of totality as he greets the film that is about to begin. Divarication of ground lies solely in capital, a pure denudation of *mimesis*, a filmic erosion of desire. All the configurations of *phainesthai* are laid bare in the *thea* of apparition, which points to a desire exceeding representation, to reason sifted into the abstraction of a necessary mode of judging, one that is "historical" without being ideological.

Perhaps Fassbinder addresses a new history with the question of imagination's despair. This *Wunderkind* of the new German cinema disengages the "free play" of imagination from the historic reality of national socialism. The irony of the film, however, lies in the intensity of illusion Hermann Hermann is engaged in, which draws *die Bewegung* into a filmic mirage of absence. Thus, Hitler is not destroyed in the imagery. His image is lifted out of the historic movement of national socialism, without exiting from the aesthetic trajectory, which mirrors the seductive distortions of Hermann's mind. Does filming here fall out of its "own" site of judgment into an "errant de-lighting"? Is Fassbinder's *Despair* a perilous deflection from our understanding of filming, that is, filming as the denuding of the history and essence of *mimesis*? While it seems that Fassbinder unwittingly disrupts the center of imagination so as to leave no trace of an ethical order, his filmic irony shows what the viewer does not want to see: time without *ethos* or finality. And, in that light, he is advancing a shadowing of time which is indeed inseparable from a radical displacement of representation. In turn, his film is haunted by the conjunction of an epochal de-lighting and de-shadowing of *mimesis*. His *mise-en-scène* provides a phenomenal mirroring of concern and disinterest.

In his later films, particularly *Germany in Autumn*, *The Marriage of Maria Braun*, and *Berlin Alexanderplatz*, a stronger sense for social interests surfaces. Few of Fassbinder's later films actually grant a radical opening for filming, since they are still drawn to a politico-ideological proclivity. This is not the case, however, in such films as *The Bitter Tears of Petra von Kant* and *Despair*, in which the attempt is made to break out of the ideological system in order to unleash a narrative terrain of fantasy. What concerns us here, of course, is *Despair*, a film, which, perhaps against Fassbinder's own efforts, flouts the representational codes of his later works, and, more importantly, a film which tests the limits of imagination. This is clearly shown in the protagonist's attempts to abandon Fassbinder's own frame of ordering: "We are making a film here," he delights in saying as *Despair* ends. Defying the order of the frame in which representation is anchored, *Despair* invites filming to begin as the film ends. Totality, now transposed into the event of image, opens the frame whose order of *mimesis* vanishes as capital shifts its luminous course to apparition. Hermann Hermann is coming out of the camera, out of the spatial limitations of the frame, into the light of judgment, where "filming is about to begin."

Conversely, Werner Herzog's aphasic sensitivity is a far cry from Fassbinder's distinctive and elegant verbal narratives. The frame is seduced by a *thea* of judgment in which discourse begins as the image fades. While discourse is just as important to Herzog as to Fassbinder's diegetic, its aesthetic function is different. For Fassbinder, discourse enunciates the illusion of pictorial presence, and supplements the disruptive development of images without digressing from the imaginal trajectory in the film. For Herzog, discourse frequently challenges the fleeting presence of images inside the frame, and turns against this order in a new vision of judgment illuminated on the screen. Herzog terrorizes the order of the frame, which delimits images and distorts their relation to language. For him, discourse explodes the frame, making it possible to align the images free of dialectic constraints with the power of the open, the *thea* of judgment. To see the images now is to stand in the proximity of discourse, so that both narrative and imagery may be regarded as belonging together in the *thea* of a new opening. No comfort emerges in this quest for unlimitedness. What shines forth in the tracking shots of Herzog's film is the *Zerissenheit* of subjectivity, the strife of *mimesis* resonating in Kaspar Hauser's phrase: "I am withdrawn from all things."[5] Filming is therefore in consonance with the director's motif of withdrawal. This is not a mystical flight into transcendence, but an *entrée* into capital, a site of judgment that unravels the beautiful-in-nature.

Herzog's prolonged static shots of fields of grass draw attention to the beautiful-in-nature not as pastoral beauty but as a different kind of seeing. Here, as in Adorno's aesthetic reflections, natural beauty signifies a "stepping out into the open."[6] To advance this idea, Herzog appropriates images of nature without submitting to a "romanticism of nature." The landscape is there to illuminate the open, whose beauty is found neither in society nor in nature but only in a trajectory of judgment which marks "first nature," or *phainesthai*. Throughout the film, Kaspar Hauser remains exiled in a world whose image is ensnared (*verfallen*) by social order. He describes coming into this order as "a terrible fall," a film of nature, a "filming" of unchanneled perception. Here representation falls into systematization as the silence of nature escapes into screaming. Everything is decopied, captured in a frame, delimited by social *mimesis*. Intentionality determines the film of existence, from "filming's" initial Socratic presence to technology's second "filming" of ground. Hence, Herzog continually attempts to de-represent conventional representations.

Filming resists the recurring genealogical moments of first (dialectical) and second ("photo-ontic") "filming," by attending to images which do not represent things or appearances but fade into a *thea* of judgment, a filming on the film of order. Not determined by Kaspar Hauser or any subject, *thea* reveals filming's site of judging, concealed by Socratic and "photo-ontic filming." The site of the end of man emerges as the beginning of judgment (*Ur-teil*). Surflectants of capital, discursive "subjects," then "appear" in a distinctive shining, a filming of vibrant spaces dissolving in apparition.

Herzog alludes to the dawn of filming in a scene of Kaspar Hauser's mountain dream, perhaps the most striking moment in the film. In these few instants of filmic disruption, filming announces a new mode of judging, a thinking which shatters the reflective mirror of subject, whose principle of ground dissipates in silence as images step out of representation to seek freedom in the *thea* of judgment. There, in the power of *phainesthai*, in the "authorial" apparition of capital, discourse begins anew.

Herzog's quest for a radically different discursive event points beyond imaginal freedom toward an opening that is always already the image that turns against all imaging, the abyss, which no filmic image conveys. A unique scene pertains to the question of apparition, to capital's falling from appearance. Herzog intensifies the import of this fall by concealing capital in the dream image of Kaspar Hauser's discourse. "It seems that my appearance has vanished," he says. Moments later, "And there is something I still need to mention. I see it clearly before my eyes" (*multi homines, pauci viri*). The focus is on *homines sapientes* rising above ground in a mist of images, lifting their faces toward the end of man. In an instance, the sun illuminates the beauty of nature, whose image the viewer recalls from an earlier scene where a swan wades out of time. A stern wind begins to blow and trees bend without will. Nothing triumphs, everything withdraws. The image dances with the missing as it sees itself coming into light, a groundless shining, a fading of power from capital, a falling of capital from power. What tarries is *phainesthai*, an illuminative play of surflectants, a new "order" of spacing, a filming whose discourse lies in the caravan of reason. Herzog's filmic event indicates only the beginning of a trajectory of judgment, seen more clearly in filming.

MADNESS AT THE END OF A FILM

A singular cultural perspective on filming, which narrows the reflective elasticity of this concept considerably, is inaugurated by Leni Riefenstahl in her film, *Triumph of the Will*. Here, filming is limited to the intoxicating presence of a concrete national symbol. *Die Bewegung* belongs to the *Beweggrund* of the spirit of the S.A. And the historical showing that the Nuremberg party rally represents is a mere function of the will of a political subject. Filming occurs, no doubt, in the narrow channeling toward presence, in Riefenstahl's case, a degrounding of ground echoing the principle of the same. It entangles itself in the ideological chaos of the Hitlerian image. Thus, Hitler himself directs *Triumph of the Will* as well as the movement of national socialism. Indeed, this very film is Hitler's *phainesthai* of "the movement." With more than one hundred technicians and the twisted genius of Goebbels, Riefenstahl produced a *thea* sui generis, of a particular political space. The open nature of filming is covered by a martial spirit of gravity. Representation is demarginalized. Countless images of cheering crowds serve the beauty of order. What is believed to be beautiful is deceptively enhanced by a peculiar constellation of music, images, and discourse. Diversely uniformed bands play lofty marches among close-ups of swastika-flags blowing toward majestic clouds. Numerous discursive practices of madness are "felt" to be the essence of the party, that total and serious image of a nation regrounded. In one scene, Hitler's attack on "the fleeting image" of socio-political concerns assigns a comic tone to his belief in the eternal symbol of the movement, whose national myth is but a shadow of the "stasis" of western culture.

For Riefenstahl, however, *Triumph of the Will* is not only a Wagnerian enshrinement of Hitler but also a filmic celebration of an age whose image has become trapped inside the political laughter of madness. The final scene of the film shows that only a certain kind of laughter triumphs in this historically late regrounding of the will: a laughter heard through the excessive bellowing of the movement, a laughter that saves the image from the domination of a diseased political imagination. Ironically, this is a laughter concealed in the self-satisfied smile of Hitler, whose very image disrupts the intentions of Goebbels' propaganda precisely because the image shows that all is a show, that all are puppets on the string of mad puppeteers. Quite simply, Hitler views filming as *his* singular space of presence, a shining that protects and maintains "the movement." For him, there is ultimately no difference between filming and *die Bewegung*. The show and what is shown are inextricable. Anything that happens will be justified as belonging to the "fixed pole" of the identity of national socialism.

As we penetrate the "film" in the mode of *filmen*, it becomes clear that what triumphs in the end of the film is not the will to power in its Hitlerian image, but the laughter that breaks the image which dominates the movement.[7] What triumphs, then, is filming against the mad "filming" of securing another ground, another presence, another mythical being. Riefenstahl shares the event of this laughter in the final scene of the film, where Hitler is shown to play out the filmic event of his own imaginal explosion. Goebbels seems to have been aware of this emotive de-lighting peculiar to Hitler's own discursive gestures of vanity, comfort, and excessive grounding. Still, the film was authorized to be shown to a people who were thought to be incapable of discerning Riefenstahl's singular aesthetic turn away from the very will of the movement. There is no doubt that in the final scene, in which Hitler elevates the "spirituality" of Nuremberg's conventional spectacle, a strong but subtle sense of disbelief in the very words of the *Führer* flashes across the screen into the perjured eyes of a film actor presuming to play a historical game later to become systematically real and unfilmable. The final image is not of a subject but of a movement whose *Beweggrund* lies in representation gone astray. The laughter concealed in the ecstatic technique of Hitlerian discourse is not that of a person but of a will whose triumph is celebrated exceedingly, as it unknowingly falls from reason.

Already, at the beginning of the documentary, Riefenstahl's montage of rooftop scenes prompts the viewer's "critical" sense of judgment. It is no accident that the film should end with a scene which echoes an initial skepticism toward a movement of the will deemed to be *the* movement of power. Riefenstahl employs the technical expertise and whatever is at her disposal to rupture the enframed identity of this film in order to evoke a radically different conquest than that of the Nuremberg party convention. Replete with images of loyalty to a cause whose ground moves outside of reason, the film, however, also assumes a commingling of images with a mode of seeing, a *thea* of judgment that has no place whatsoever in the movement. Riefenstahl, therefore, begins to announce a filming that is still mythical in character but no longer solely national in its social manifestation. Her quest for a site withdrawn from a mimetic, that is, a historical, reflection of ground is brought to fruition in an earlier project, *The Blue Light*. There, the beautiful-in-nature (*das Naturschöne*) exceeds the alpine landscape, as appears in Junta's stepping out into the light, into the open, into a composure of judging where filming can begin to shine beyond a plurality of filmic prejudgments.

Between Heidegger and Adorno: Hitchcock's 'Kehre'

In addition to instances of the new German cinema, there is a sense in which Hitchcock's *Vertigo* serves to indicate "another beginning" for filming. Few films study the relation of filming and judgment as carefully as this particular film. One could even say that *Vertigo*, when it is read on a geneafilmic level, reveals imagination wandering within a circle of decentering turns in judgment. Between reason and madness, exhibited in the relation of John Ferguson and Madeleine Elster, there emerges a consistent filmic *lethe*, which Hitchcock strives but fails to overcome. What lingers at the end of the film is the inevitable withdrawal of the supersensible. And yet, from the beginning to the end, Hitchcock's film tells the "story" of Madeleine, who appears/dis-appears in a filmic form of apparition. While Madeleine herself is never there (in the frame), a hauntingly brilliant and eloquent appearing of Corlotta Valdes, solely in the image of a portrait, eclipses the self of Judy in Madeleine and, finally, Madeleine in Judy. Hitchcock, unable to throw off the apparitional power of Corlotta, awakens filmmaking to a filming or mode of judging that is ever questioning, ever open to the vertiginous movements of imagination on the cinematic screen of art. With Gavin Elster, he waits for something to appear that does not exist, while John Ferguson's contemplative wandering is comforted by the thought: "There's an answer for everything." Hitchcock's film holds up a promise of apparition, an elegant constellation of fantasy and reality in which a "different beginning," indeed, another way of thinking, is possible. From a metaphysical perspective, his project fails, because what lingers in the film and at the end is a felling, a falling, that is, a filming of what lies at the heart of this film, namely, the desire for the supersensible to appear, if not a desperate demand for such an appearance. That filming, as we name it, does not demand nor necessarily desire such a dimension, does not diminish the significance of Hitchcock's attempt to aspire, if you will, to a mode of filming in which apparition suddenly rises and falls from the everyday world. Without knowing it, Hitchcock seems to nourish an important aspect of Adorno's "aesthetic" explorations: "While apparition is the instant of illumination and of being touched by something, the image is the paradoxical attempt to capture this exceedingly fleeting moment" (*AT*, 125). The attempt to make the image stand still, and simultaneously to intensify the dynamic quality of this desirable stillness, fails in the cinema, and yet, it fares well in filming. Hence, the supplementary shining or apparition that rises in each instance of the film, but does not present itself in the film as such, endures in filming as judgment wanders through the diverse configurations of color, music, and discourse.

Diverging from William Rothman's intriguing reading of *Vertigo*,[8] I am highlighting a geneafilmic account of the film which underscores in particular the post-aesthetic relation of reason and madness brought to light in Madeleine's "apparitional" affinity to her beloved. Madeleine, always at a distance, always departing, always falling from view, appears exceedingly disruptive in every moment of the film, because she exhibits what cannot be seen, what cannot and will not be in the sensible world of the cinema. A post-aesthetic signifier, Madeleine draws madness into reason, discerning the limits of a playful suspension of judging. The subject is no longer a designatable being, but suddenly fades into silence. The narrative in the film becomes problematic insofar as Madeleine, as "image" of a work of art on its way toward apparition, cannot participate in the ontic strategies of Elster, Ferguson, or even Hitchcock. Free of completing the metaphor of her being, she falls from Hitchcock's own filming. Between being and apparition, Madeleine appears as an *Eräugnis* without a comprehensive form. Initially, directed by Hitchcock, Madeleine meets the "other" Heidegger in Gavin Elster, who attempts to bind her to the filmic deception of his "ontic" scheme. Steering away from what she is not, Madeleine wanders about with Scottie in an Adornoian search for the spirit in the work of art. Resisting her allegiance to the "other" Heidegger, Madeleine is always already "outside" the political dream of reason that is "inside" a post-aesthetic vertigo of filming. "Whipped along, spinning, twirling faster and faster until matter shatters into pieces, crumbles into dust,"[9] Madeleine appears as a work of art that does not exist, a *Heimat* which the "other" Heidegger never allows himself to see except in his text. The turn which overturns the *Kehre* during the 1930s does not end in the blind alley of political sameness. Madeleine frees herself from the "other" Heidegger as she opens the cinematic images for Scottie's vertigo, corresponding in part to Adorno's disruptive aesthetic judgment concerning truth in art. Scottie, however, while pursuing Madeleine, is still driven by the *idea* of Madeleine, which for Hitchcock becomes increasingly difficult to communicate. Indeed, the film turns the idea of a single dialectic upside down, insofar as Madeleine emerges as an indiscernible work of art yet to signify a disruptive sight for discerning.[10] As Madeleine's eye glances between the texts of Heidegger and Adorno, close to the edges of a mirrorless judging (*Ur-teil*), an anti-art surfaces in the domain of art, turning post-aesthetically to apparition, a vertiginous gap saturating the myth of *mimesis*. "Just wandering about . . . and where were you before? And what were you doing there? Just wandering about . . ."[11] At the end of the corridor of reflection, Madeleine's itinerary of thought conveys the irony of metaphysics, which whirls dizzily in a post-aesthetic space between Heidegger's home (*Heimat*) and Adorno's *promesse du bonheur*. While filming is no longer wedded to a *Dasein* at home in essentiality, it also does not provide a promise that is metaphysically speculative. Thus, it falls from Heidegger's countermetaphysical narrative of truth as well as from Adorno's aesthetic speculum of hope. In a shapeless flux, it wanders about, curling the text along the margins of thought into a whirl of judging.

Between Heidegger and Adorno lies the bed of another text, a new literature of Madeleine, a post-aesthetic fantasy of filming. Burdened with the memory of reason's frozen rules, Madeleine plays freely in the house of *ethos*, as the story of Athens ends. Hovering in between the forgottenness of being and the dream of another home, Madeleine swirls around moments of judgment, gazing night and day at the city of freedom; whence she breaks with the city of wisdom and falls in love with San Francisco, the end of metaphysical origins.

> Wandering far from all mankind, condemned
> to forage in the wilderness like wolves,
> pursue your fate, chaotic souls, and flee
> the infinite you bear within yourselves! (*FM*, 129)

Far from tender and tyrannous Hollywood images, the work of art yet to be scatters its breath into the air of a northern *eros*, the city of Madeleine. There in the light, without a dwelling, she gazes upon a newly born poet filming the story of Zarathustra's "laughing lion." Between Heidegger and Adorno, the overman sings again; this time not in the form of another man, but an overturning, a vertigo, the maddening tune of a different death, a dialectic dying without the ashes of a god, an unimaginable glowing, a deframing of the pale shadows of a sluggish subject, a luminous wandering beyond the familiar slums of philosophy's dark terrain.

One of Hitchcock's unique epistemic achievements in the film is his ability to distinguish between apparition in a post-aesthetic shining of "another beginning" and existence as the unsophisticated return of the same. Granted, apparition merely begins to show the post-aesthetic turns of judgment in *Vertigo*, unlike his other films, this one reveals little interest in the human subject per se. Instead, what is invariably at play in the filmic movement of desire is what withdraws from images altogether. In *Vertigo*, reason and madness are syncopated. Their displacement, however, is merely temporary. Hitchcock's allusions to white towers, churches, and nuns defrock judgment from the "privilege" of "aesthetic" freedom, thereby linking apparition to ontic religious anchorings. What does appear exceedingly in apparition goes up in smoke at the end of the film, when the silhouetted figure turns out to be a nun. Here, neither a ghost nor a free shining embraces the images that might serve to indicate where judgment shall turn next in the attempt to think "another beginning." What begins as an illuminating account of filming, wandering freely from *Kehre* to *Kehre* in judgment's post-aesthetic itinerary, culminates in a tragic "vertigo" of possible religious consciousness, a lapse from filming, yet still (belonging to) a mode of *filmen*.

'VERTIGO,' 'VERTERE,' 'FILMEN,' FILMING

Filming surfaces as *filmen*,[12] an imaginal showing of judgment's turn from political blind spots, a cinematic attempt to deframe power. In this context, *filmen* serves to underline a disruption of metaphysical reason and its analogical (technical) relay, mere filmmaking. It exceeds "filming" understood as a dialectic screening of being, and throws off the protective cloak of becoming which had always been the mark of metaphysics. *Filmen*, the "altarity" within filming, evokes "aspects of otherness" beyond otherness.[13] Its cinematic difference broaches filming in the wake of a postmodern operation of judgment. Still, *filmen* is merely the beginning of filming, in which a "disjunctive" mode of judging reveals a filmic turn, a vertigo which distracts from the fascinations of intense ideological movements. The cinematic technology limits the possibilities of imaginal dehiscence. And while filming initially relies on the cinematic operation of *filmen*, it exceeds this technique as it recedes from the imaginal movements of world, a displaced site in which political illusions abound.[14]

Filming sketches out relays of thought without restricting judgment to a movement of images enframed by a particular cause of action (*Beweggrund*). It relinquishes the thespian inclination of a thinking that festoons judgment with drapes of uncontrolled images. Robbing distraction of its meaning, filming reveals a nonimaginal relation of judgment, a radical spiralling of *Kehre*. A different turn surfaces, a vertigo which films out disoriented metaphysical (political) views and dislodges Heidegger's turn to an aesthetic force of politicized images.[15]

Thinking, which is now no longer exhibited as an "alluring heir" to a dialectic of political presence, radically deframes any connection to a *Beweggrund* of problematic aspirations. The filmic scene provides no photoplays of a confused political imagination, but does end the distracting *Kehre* toward discursive elations on the beauty of the state. The nostalgia for the tempting illusions of essence vanishes as filming disrupts the aesthetic pleasures of a metaphysically justified elevation of history. The new vertigo does not turn to *eidos*, to a principle or formidable idea which keeps alive the "photo-ontic" enticement of ground in a limited *Weltanschauung*; instead it rises above the myth of *mimesis* while descending from the enthusiasm for a political legitimacy of the principle of ground.[16]

A frameless, non-mimetic hovering occurs between position and negation, as capital drifts to an imperceptible *phainesthai*. What is vertiginous in filming is indeed capital, that sublime site of judgment without the will for images. No place of repose, capital evaporates the dialectic reflection of production and enables judgment to wander freely from *Kehre* in the filmic scene of apparition. Endowed as filming is with capital, it does not command a particular mode of thought or action, since no relation within the frame of relations is imputed to capital. "Postmodern" *lumen naturale*, filming breaks out of critique between Heidegger's clearing and Adorno's utopic glimpses of a world free of fear. While its thinking does not impose itself, it cannot forget the crematoria of a Maidanek, whose images evoke the violence of political presence. Accordingly, filming may open up fruitful avenues of investigation with perspectives "that displace and estrange the world, [that] reveal it to be, with its rifts and crevices, as indigent and distorted as it will appear one day in the messianic light."[17]

Notes

◆

INTRODUCTION

1. It is important to bear in mind that Heidegger's use of the word *Ge-stell* may refer to both the risks and the possibilities of today's technological world. He does not employ this word in a negative sense as is sometimes thought. In our study, *Ge-stell* is employed as a distinctive shining, a "technical" bursting open of being, a filmic event which cannot be negated. Our application of this word, therefore, exceeds but is not in conflict with Heidegger's account of *Ge-stell*, as described in the lectures "Die Frage nach der Technik" ("The Question Concerning Technology") and "Die Kehre" ("The Turning") in *Die Technik und die Kehre* (Tübingen: Verlag Gunther Neske, 1962), 5–47. A reference to *Ge-stell* in the protocol to a seminar on the lecture "Time and Being" is of particular interest: "Es wurde nicht geklärt, wie das Ge-stell, das das Wesen der Technik ausmacht, also von etwas, das, soweit wir wissen, nur auf der Erde geschieht, ein Name für das universelle Sein sein kann" ("It was not made clear, how enframing as essence of technology, which, as far as we know, happens only on earth, can be a name for universal being": my translation). *Zur Sache des Denkens* (Tübingen: Max Niemeyer Verlag, 1969), 35.
2. Rene Descartes, *Discourse on Method and Meditations on First Philosophy*, trans. D. A. Cress (Indianapolis: Hackett, 1980), 61.
3. Compare Heidegger's discussion of *das anfängliche Denken* ("originary thinking") in *Beiträge zur Philosophie* (Frankfurt am Main: Vittorio Klostermann, 1989), 55–83.
4. "Eidos"—"idea," underlines a "showing" and a "seeing" of this "showing." With regard to Plato's philosophy, it is inadequate to set apart the notional from the imaginal. "Das Bild," writes Rudolf Eucken in alluding to the Platonic dialectic, "gesellt sich zum Begriff und verschmilzt mit ihm zu einer untrennbaren Einheit" ("The image socializes with the concept and blends into an inseparable unity": my translation). *Geschichte der Philosophischen Terminologie* (Leipzig, 1879), 19. See Heidegger's 1937/38 lecture *Grundfragen der Philosophie* (Frankfurt am Main: Vittorio Klostermann, 1984), 68, for an account of an "imaginal" understanding of *idea*. Also, Heidegger's "Wissenschaft und Besinnung," in *Vorträge und Aufsätze* (Pfullingen: Gunther Neske, 1954), 52–56.

   While in a Greek apprehending of presence, world is not image enframed by images, Heidegger insists that "the beingness of whatever is, defined for Plato as *eidos* (*Aussehen*, "view"), is the presupposition, destined far in advance and long ruling indirectly in concealment, for the world's having to become image" (*QCT*, 131).

5. See Martin Heidegger, *Grundfragen der Philosophie* (Frankfurt am Main: Vittorio Klostermann, 1984), 105.

6. See Martin Heidegger, "On the Being and Conception of *Physis* in Aristotle's *Physics* B 1," trans. T. J. Sheehan, *Man and World* 9, no. 3 (August 1976), 241. Here Heidegger refers to "der öffnende Vorstoss" ("the open thrust") of philosophy.

7. *Ab-grund* literally means "withdrawing from ground" and is translated as abyss, precipice, or chasm. Our focus on *Ab-grund* entails a radical critique of ground and a sense of freeing reason *from* ground as dialectical principle *for* the open "abyss" of filming. See Heidegger's account of the question concerning the relation of *Grund* and *Ab-grund* in the lecture "Vom Wesen des Grundes," in *Wegmarken* (Frankfurt am Main: Vittorio Klostermann, 1976), 123–75. In this lecture, Heidegger writes: "Als *dieser* Grund aber ist die Freiheit der *Ab-grund* des Daseins" ("But as *this* ground, freedom is the *abyss* of *Dasein*": my translation) (174). Hence, Heidegger's genealogical reading of the principle of ground is supplemented by a distinctive emphasis on freedom, indeed, freedom *from* ground: "*Die Freiheit ist der Grund des Grundes*" ("*Freedom is the ground of the ground*") (174).

8. See Stanley Cavell, *The World Viewed* (Cambridge: Harvard University Press, 1979); Timothy Corrigan, *The Displaced Image* (Austin: University of Texas Press, 1983); Gilles Deleuze, *Cinema 1, The Movement-Image*, trans. H. Tomlinson and B. Habberjam (Minneapolis: University of Minnesota Press, 1986), and *Cinema 2, The Time-Image*, trans. H. Tomlinson and R. Galeta (Minneapolis: University of Minnesota Press, 1989); Eric Rentschler (ed.), *German Film and Literature* (New York and London: Methuen, 1986); William Rothman, *The "I" of the Camera* (Cambridge: Cambridge University Press, 1988).

9. See Brigitte Peucker's fine article, "Werner Herzog, in Quest of the Sublime," in *New German Filmmakers*, ed. Klaus Phillips (New York: Frederick Unger, 1984), 168–94.

10. Filming serves as "witness" to the "tearing apart" (*Zerissenheit*) of *Zeit* and *Geist*. It is a distinctive seeing of the rupture between time and reason.

11. For a rich exploration of *phainesthai*, see Martin Heidegger, *Sein und Zeit* (Tübingen: Max Niemeyer Verlag, 1967), 28–34. In some respect, *phainesthai* provides the framework in which I cast my reading of filming. Still, filming no longer shines *at* or *forth*, owing to the epistemic dissimulation and silencing (*Verwerfung*) of the principle of ground.

12. Immanuel Kant, *Critique of Pure Reason*, trans. N. K. Smith (New York: St. Martin's Press, 1965), 146.

13. For instance, filming, in the sense I wish to use this word, comes closer to the idea of *vernehmen* ("becoming aware") rather than *vorstellen* ("representing"). Indeed, filming as an immediate receiving, a becoming aware of presence, films out "filming" conceived of as a representing which arrests and objectifies things.

   Throughout this text *Gelassenheit* is translated as "com-posure," which retains a sense of *Gelassenheit's* "freeing" and "letting-be," but also inserts a mode of posing or setting in place which filming captures. In the text, "com-posure" is aligned to a Heideggerian moment of *Gellasenheit* and participates in a process of letting that moment be. Filming, however, exceeds *phainesthai* in its subversive depresencing.

14. Compare Martin Heidegger, *Was Heisst Denken?* (Tübingen: Max Niemeyer Verlag, 1971), 141. Heidegger points to the importance of a renewed (imaginal) seeing: "What has been seen can never be proved by adducing reasons and counter-reasons. Such a procedure overlooks what is decisive—the looking. If what is seen is put in words, its mention by name can never compel the seeing look. At best, it can offer a token of what a seeing look, renewed again and again, would presumably show more clearly": *What Is Called Thinking* (New York: Harper & Row, 1968), 233. In his lecture on "Die Kehre," Heidegger refers to this "seeing look" (*blicken*) as "the essential glance of being" (*QCT*, 49). Also, compare Werner Marx, *Heidegger*, ed. H. G. Gadamer, W. Marx, C. F. v. Weizsäcker (Freiburg/München: Verlag Karl Alber, 1977), 18.
15. See Heidegger, *Die Technik und die Kehre*, 43–44.

CHAPTER 1. NIETZSCHE AND THE PROBLEM OF GROUND

1. Friedrich Nietzsche, *Die Geburt der Tragödie*, in *Werke in Drei Bänden* (Stuttgart: Europaeischer Buchklub, 1966), 37.
2. *Seven Famous Greek Plays*, ed. Whitney J. Oates and Eugene O'Neill (New York: Random House, 1950), 182.
3. Ibid., 175.
4. Friedrich Nietzsche, *On the Genealogy of Morals*, tr. Walter Kaufmann (New York: Vintage Books, 1969), 78.
5. "With every real growth in the whole, the 'meaning' of the individual organs also changes; in certain circumstances their partial destruction, a reduction in their numbers (for example, through the disappearance of intermediary numbers) can be a sign of increasing strength and perfection. It is not too much to say that even a partial *diminution of utility*, an atrophying and degeneration, a loss of meaning and purposiveness, in short, death—is among the conditions of an actual *progressus*, which always appears in the shape of a will and way to *greater power* and is always carried through at the expense of numerous smaller powers" (*GM*, 78). Also compare "Eine neue Denkweise—welche immer eine neue Messweise ist . . ." ("A new manner of thinking—which is invariably a new mode of measuring . . .": my translation) in *Werke, Kritische Gesamtausgabe*, ed. G. Colli and M. Montinari (Berlin: Walter de Gruyter, 1974), VII, 3:227.
6. "Being new, nameless, hard to understand, we premature births of an as yet unproven future need for a new goal also a new means—namely, a new health, stronger, more seasoned, tougher, more audacious, and gayer than any previous health": *The Gay Science*, tr. Walter Kaufmann (New York: Vintage Books, 1974), 346. "The involuntariness of image and metaphor is strangest of all; one no longer has any notion of what is an image or a metaphor: everything offers itself as the nearest, most obvious, simplest expression. It actually seems, to allude to something Zarathustra says, as if the things themselves approached and offered themselves as metaphors" (*Ecce Homo* in *GM*, 301).
7. Compare "Zarathustra's Prologue" in *The Portable Nietzsche*, tr. Walter Kaufmann (New York: Viking Press, 1968), 121.
8. John Sallis, *Spacings—of Reason and Imagination* (Chicago: The University of Chicago Press, 1987), xiii.
9. Friedrich Nietzsche, *The Will to Power*, tr. Walter Kaufmann (New York: Vintage Books, 1968), 504.

10. Friedrich Nietzsche, "Multum in parvo. Eine Philosophie im Auszug" (*Werke*: *Kritische Gesamtausgabe*), VII, 3:344.
11. "Der Wille zur Macht als Leben: Höhepunkt des historischen *Selbstbewusstseins*" (*Werke*: *Kritische Gesamtausgabe*, VIII 3:299.
12. *On the Genealogy of Morals and Ecce Homo*, tr. Walter Kaufmann (New York: Vintage Books, 1969), 327.
13. "Mein Trost ist, dass alles, was war, ewig ist": *The Will to Power*, 548.
14. Ibid., 422.
15. *Werke*: *Kritische Gesamtausgabe*, VIII, 3:166.
16. *Gelassenheit* of imagination does not occur until Heidegger radically questions the principle of ground.
17. Compare John Sallis, *Spacings—of Reason and Imagination*, xiv.
18. Friedrich Nietzsche, *Beyond Good and Evil*, tr. Walter Kaufmann (New York: Vantage Books, 1966), 25.
19. Friedrich Nietzsche, *On the Advantage and Disadvantage of History for Life*, tr. Peter Preuss (Indianapolis: Hackett Publishing Co.), 22.
20. Ibid., 15.
21. *On the Genealogy of Morals*, 77.

CHAPTER 2. POSTMODERNISM'S SHORT LETTER, PHILOSOPHY'S LONG FAREWELL

1. Cf. Theodor Adorno, *In Search of Wagner*, trans. Rodney Livingstone (Manchester: NLB, 1981), 143–56.
2. "Husserl says of the living word that it is a *geistige Leiblichkeit*, a spiritual flesh" (*M*, 82). "See Edmund Husserl's *Phantasie, Bildbewusstsein, Erinnerung (1898–1925)* (The Hague: Martinus Nijhoff, 1980), 540.
3. Modernity's resistance, particularly Baudelaire's poetry of the sublime, grazes the political principle of ground with elegant despair. In pursuit of aesthetic pleasure, Baudelaire thinks the end of modernity at the limit of the presence of power: "Elsewhere! Too far, too late, or never at all! Of me you know nothing, I nothing of you—you whom I might have loved and who knew that too!" (*FM*, 98). Nevertheless, such poetic doubt of high modernity's transition to political presence belongs to a modernist dialectic of interiority. This lyric poet in the era of high capitalism, as Benjamin calls Baudelaire, is still seduced by the intensity of presence, albeit a disruptively aesthetic presence complicitous with Nietzsche's de-politicized thought.
4. F. R. Dallmayr, *Twilight of Subjectivity* (Amherst: Massachusetts Institute of Technology Press, 1983), 134.
5. Cf. John Sallis, "Imagination and the Meaning of Being," in *Heidegger et l'idée de la phénoménologie*, by Volp et al. (Dordrecht, Netherlands: Kluwer Academic Publishers, 1988), 127–44. Also compare Gilles Deleuze, *Cinema 1, L'Image--Mouvement* (Paris: Minuit, 1983). While Deleuze clarifies cinematic images and sign, he does not examine the question of a postmodern relation between imagination and "filming."
6. For a critique of postmodern "dis-positions" of the self, see Jurgen Habermas, *The Philosophical Discourse of Modernity*, trans. Frederick Lawrence (Cambridge, Mass.: MIT Press, 1987), 83–105, 238–65. For a more detailed inquiry into the question of "pure modernity," compare David Kolb, *The Critique of*

Pure Modernity (Chicago: University of Chicago Press, 1987).

7. Later on in the text we will see that filming diverges from a "process of images," proceeding to an operation of what may be called "image-disruption."

8. See Jean Baudrillard, "Ecstasy of Communication," in *The Anti-Aesthetic,* ed. Hal Foster (Port Townsend, Washington: Bay Press, 1983), 126–33.

9. See Timothy Corrigan, *The Displaced Image* (Austin: University of Texas Press, 1983), 3–23.

10. John Sallis, *The Gathering of Reason* (Athens: Ohio University Press, 1980), xii.

11. Jean-Francois Lyotard, *The Postmodern Condition: A Report on Knowledge* (Minneapolis: University of Minnesota Press, 1984), 15.

12. Cf. Sallis, "Imagination and the meaning of Being," 130.

13. *The Gathering of Reason,* 176.

14. *Proceedings of American Catholic Philosophical Association (ACPA),* April 1978, 75.

15. *The Gathering of Reason,* 176.

16. Ibid.

17. Ibid.; *Proceedings of ACPA,* 65.

18. "Der Überstieg zur Welt ist die Freiheit selbst" ("The step over to world is freedom itself"). Martin Heidegger, "Vom Wesen des Grundes," in *Wegmarken* (Frankfurt am Main: Vittorio Klostermann, 1976), 163.

19. *Ab-grund* denotes ground withdrawn from ground as principle of reason: "*Die Freiheit ist der Grund des Grundes. Als dieser Grund aber ist die Freiheit der Ab-grund des Daseins*" ("*Freedom is the ground of the ground.* But as this ground, freedom is the *abyss of Dasein*") *(WG,* 174).

20. "Das Aufbrechen des Abgrundes in der gründenden Transzendenz ist vielmehr die Urbewegung, die die Freiheit mit uns selbst vollzieht . . ." ("The opening of the abyss in the grounding transcendence is rather the primal movement, which freedom carries out with us . . .": my translation) *(WG,* 174).

21. "So bildet das Bild den Ort des entbergenden Bergens (der *Aletheia*")" *(ED,* 121).

22. In *Vom Wesen der Wahrheit* (1930), Heidegger discusses the question of ground from the horizon of an antifoundationalist theory of freedom. He writes: "Die Freiheit ist als das Seinlassen des Seienden in sich das entschlossene, d. h. das sich nicht verschliessende Verhältnis" ("As the letting-be of beings, freedom is the resolute relation, i. e., one that is not self-secluding": my translation) *(WG,* 194). To think freedom as the relation that does not close or enframe world as image is to prepare the way for a *phainesthai* displaced from ground. The abyss of this relation is the condition for a possible grounding. Hence, a sense of nostalgia for origin can still be found in the operation of Heidegger's de-limiting of ground. Nonetheless, what seems inevitable in the "free play" of imagination is the very trembling of the thought of *Wesen,* so that *Anwesen* or presence comes into presence as *Un-wesen,* as *mimesis* that "gives" but does not take. This mimetic de-grounding conceals the origin of ground. There is no origin as such. There is merely shining, lighting, filmic modes of *phainesthai* in which world belongs to the event of image.

23. So Heidegger writes: "Discourse lets us see something from the very thing which discourse is about": *Being and Time,* trans. J. Macquarrie and E. Robinson (New York: Harper & Row, 1962), 56.

24. From a genealogical perspective, Heidegger may be called the philosopher of filming. With regard to *phainesthai,* he remarks: "No word has caused as much havoc and confusion in philosophy as this one" *(HCT,* 81).

25. The "subversive de-lighting" of filming consists in extruding the "phaos" of the dialectic from the possibility of imposing another metaphysical constraint upon the faculty of judgment. A trace of "de-lighting" can be discerned in Heidegger's reference to a precise task: "Der Versuch, Sein ohne das Seiende zu denken, wird notwendig" ("The attempt to think being without beings will be necessary"). *Zur Sache des Denken* (Tübingen: Max Niemeyer Verlag, 1969), 2.
26. The phrase is Feuerbach's (from *The Essence of Christianity*), but see Susan Sontag, *On Photography* (New York: Penguin, 1977), 153.
27. Such a confrontation of "absolute nothingness" is revealed in Nietzsche's "death of God" proposition, a sublime challenge to imagination's power of judgment.
28. "The Grounding of the Modern World Image by Metaphysics" came to be known as "Die Zeit des Weltbildes," in *Holzwege* (Frankfurt am Main: Vittorio Klostermann, 1977).
29. Cf. Vincent B. Leitch, *Deconstructive Criticism* (New York: Columbia University Press, 1983), 34.
30. "What Calls for Thinking?" in *Basic Writings*, trans. David F. Krell (New York: Harper & Row, 1977), 350.
31. An important aspect of the Heideggerian thematic of *Kehre* is the transition from *Ereignis* to *Eräugnis*. *Eräugnis* is derived from the archaic verb *eräugnen*, "to bring to one's eyes," "to bring to light." To my knowledge, Heidegger does not employ the word *phainesthai* in his later texts. I believe *Eräugnis* serves to underscore the "sigetic" sense of seeing in relation to the question of "the essence of technology." While *phainesthai* is still inscribed in the event of appropriation (*Ereignis*), it undergoes a more radical turn in the naming of *Eräugnis*, especially with regard to the historical disclosure of being by means of *Ge-stell*. Thus, Heidegger remarks: "Ereignis ist eignende Eräugnis" ("The event is its own seeing": my translation). *Die Technik und die Kehre* (Tübingen: Verlag Günther Neske, 1962), 44.
32. "Such magnitudes may also be called *flowing*, since the synthesis of productive imagination involved in their production is a progression in time, and the continuity of time is ordinarily designated by the term flowing or flowing away" (*CR*, 204).

CHAPTER 3. VELÁZQUEZ'S GLANCE, FOUCAULT'S SMILE

1. I propose a "non-egological" reading of Spinoza's thinking in *Nietzsche und Spinoza* (Meisenheim am Glan: Verlag Anton Hain, 1975), 152–214.
2. In relation to this "dispersion" of ground which classical thought announces, Foucault surprisingly pays little attention to the man, i. e., the visitor in the clearing. He mistakenly believes that he is about to enter the room, when it seems quite clear, by the way he stands with his right foot in front of his left on the stairway, that he is ready to leave. Indeed, this figure disfigures, so to speak, the unity of form in the painting. He takes in the scene from the back, as Foucault insists, not as someone who is eager to observe the refraction of power, but as someone who seems bewildered by the "dispersion" of the subject *in* representation. Still, it seems he is merely there to visit once more the classical space of time, as difference beckons him to step into the light which shines upon identity. He observes the figures carefully, particularly the royal subjects on the canvas enframed in the mirror he cannot see.

3. The cross was added after the completion of the painting, when the artist became a knight in 1658.

CHAPTER 4. ADORNO'S CRITIQUE OF PURE 'MIMESIS'

1. Cf. Peter Bürger, *Theory of the Avant-Garde*, trans. Michael Shaw (Minneapolis: University of Minnesota Press, 1984).

2. Is not the very concept of "work" radically questioned by modernism? Does aesthetics today dispense with the notion of "work"? In the *Critique of Judgment*, for example, Kant does not rely on the use of a concept such as "work." Instead, aesthetic judgment becomes the criterion for aesthetic experience. And what is beautiful in nature does not have the character of work for Kant. The crisis of work in modern aesthetics, however, is not limited to Kant's *Critique of Judgment*. It emerges in Hegel's aesthetics, in Heidegger's philosophy of art, as well as in Adorno's aesthetic theory. Hegel understands art as works of *phainesthai*, works of pure appearance. With regard to art, Hegel does not simply espouse imitation of spirit. In his lectures on *Aesthetics*, he writes: "What should enchant us is not the subject of the painting and its lifelikeness, but the pure appearance [*interesseloses Scheinen*], which is wholly without the sort of interest that the subject has. The one thing certain about beauty is, as it were, appearance [*Scheinen*] for its own sake, and art is mastery in the portrayal of all the secrets of this ever profounder pure appearance [*Scheinen*] of external realities" (*M*, 71–108). Work is, therefore, explored in relation to the shift from a dialectic of form and content to a phenomenology of form. And art is still viewed as work shining forth sensuousness of spirit. This aesthetic charting of *mimesis*, however, is no more than a disinterested shining-showing of imagination's work. Heidegger unleashes *Geist* when he states, in "The Origin of the Work of Art," that the nature of art lies in the work of art. Work (*Werk*) is the disclosure of truth at work in art. It is not grasped as product of imagination but as "free play" of truth in the open terrain of imagination. Hence, works of imagination are, at least for Heidegger, works of art if truth happens to be at work in art. As a genealogical work of imagination, metaphysics may be a powerful, yet limited, art work.

3. "In Ideologie aber spielt Kunst hinüber, indem sie, *imago* von nicht Vertauschbarem, suggeriert, in der Welt wäre nicht alles vertauschbar." Adorno, *Ästhetische Theorie* (Frankfurt am Main: Suhrkamp Verlag, 1970), 128: ("By the same token, art—the *imago* of the unexchangeable—verges on ideology because it makes us believe there are things in the world that are not for exchange".) *Aesthetic Theory*, trans. C. Lenhardt (London and New York: Routledge & Kegan Paul, 1984), 123.

4. Marx's idea of the *complete* emancipation of the human senses is delimited by Adorno's aesthetic insight into the subject's *incomplete* freedom.

5. Compare *AT*, 206–10.

6. In the *Poetics*, Aristotle observes that imitation is natural to man from childhood. In fact, man is distinguished from animals because of his imitative being. For Plato, the crisis of the *polis* lies in a mimetic withdrawal from *eidos*. Socrates, who represents the image of *eidos*, is put to death by a social force that seems to have little regard for the imitation of ideas. This political defeat of *mimesis* signifies the poverty of political authority. In its natural attitude, the *polis*

discerns Plato's paradigm of tyranny—*mimesis*. But Socrates' dialectic addiction to imitation is too restrictive for the democratic government of Athens. In general, however, western thought welcomed Plato's restriction for over two millennia. Later, the dominance of the mimetic theory gave way to the hermeneutic insight of "continuity of meaning," and obversely to the genealogical concept of "discontinuity of meaning." Adaptation and duplication of the Socratic dialectic had become the norm in the history of thought, together with Adorno's negative dialectic. All that is substantive in metaphysical thought is but a *mimesis* of the principle of the highest ground—whether it be *eidos*, *hen*, God, the absolute, or *Geist*.

7. Aristotle's conception of *mimesis* occasionally deviates from Plato's. In the *Politics*, for example, Aristotle is clearly concerned with the question: "What is imitated?" This question as well as its possible answers are moral and political in nature. For Aristotle, *mimesis* is related to the practical sphere. And so is art; music, for instance, is thought to be "remedy to pain caused by toil" (*Politics*, 1339b15). Art is therefore not linked to a mere "movement of sense" but is recognized as "a transformation of the soul" by means of the movement of sense.

8. Compare *AT*, 164–72.

9. *AT*, 30. "The truly new is the concrete" (*AT*, 195). It is the particular, the sentence that may have no meaning, the image that may be entirely obscure. "Works of art have to absorb their worst enemy" (*AT*, 195) in order to get away from false concreteness. With regard to the idea of "false concreteness" in contemporary social theories, compare the illuminating text of Roberto Mangabeira Unger, *False Necessity* (New York: Cambridge University Press, 1987).

10. An interesting reading of "a semiology of the self" can be found in Hugh J. Silverman's *Inscriptions* (New York and London: Routledge & Kegan Paul, 1987).

11. *Velázquez, Goya and the Dehumanization of Art*, trans. Alexis Brown (New York: W. W. Norton & Co., 1972), 99.

12. See Jacques Derrida, *Margins of Philosophy*, tr. Alan Bass (Chicago: University of Chicago Press, 1982), 3–27.

CHAPTER 5. THE AESTHETIC FALL OF POLITICAL MODERNITY

1. The term "marxism" with the initial lower case is intentional in this text. It serves two purposes: one, it underscores the theoretical assumption of continual change in "marxist" theory; two, it indicates that this classic political theory has both theoretically and practically betrayed the progressive, disruptive views of Marx's thinking.

2. Nietzsche distinguished between the idea of a "first" and "second" nature in an early text, *Vom Nutzen und Nachteil der Historie für das Leben* (München: Carl Hanser, 1966), 230. "We implant a new habit, a new instinct, a second nature so that the first nature withers away. It is an attempt, as it were, *a posteriori* to give oneself a past from which one would like to be descended in opposition to the past from which one descended:—always a dangerous attempt because it is so difficult to find a limit in denying the past and because second natures are mostly feebler than the first". *On the Advantage and Disadvantage of History for Life*, trans. Peter Preuss (Indianapolis: Hackett Publishing Co., 1980), 22. Adorno's

use of these terms modifies Nietzsche's reference: "First nature" is "the image of freedom," longed for in the past without ever becoming actual, yet real in "second reflection." "Second nature" emerges as the historic, social epiphenomenon of "first nature," consonant with "first reflection," i. e., metaphysics. Hence, "first nature" is still the principle of hope, the *promesse du bonheur*, the beauty of nature embedded in imagination as revealed through "second reflection."

3. With regard to the importance of *Gedächtnis* in Adorno's thinking, Martin Jay notes: "Unlike Marcuse, whose concept of memory drew on Hegel's defence of *Erinnerung* as the reinternalization of something externalized, Adorno followed Benjamin in stressing the redemptive power of *Gedächtnis*, the reverential recollection of an object always prior to the remembering subject": *Adorno* (Cambridge, Mass.: Harvard University Press, 1984), 68.

4. "Denn das Naturschöne als Erscheinendes ist selber Bild" ("For natural beauty in appearing is itself image": my translation) (*AT*, 105).

5. "Works of art become works of art when they produce that surplus which is their transcendent quality" (*AT*, 116).

6. Adorno sometimes refers to this overturning disclosed in works of art as "fireworks."

7. Compare Foucault's analysis of this hypothesis with regard to a genealogy of sexuality in *The History of Sexuality, Volume I: An Introduction* (New York: Vintage, 1980), 17–35.

8. Adorno caught a glimpse of that when he warned that there is no guarantee anywhere that art will keep its promise. Cf. *AT*, 347.

9. "That is why every theory of art must also be critical of art" (*AT*, 122–23).

CHAPTER 6. TRANSGRESSING THE KANTIAN AESTHETIC

1. Transgressing the Kantian aesthetic, the beautiful denotes an "objectless world" for a power of judgment (*Urteilskraft*) that moves freely in the imaginal space of disinterestedness. Without that world, namely, imagination's *Ur-bild*, judgment would not be free for a radical disruption of representation. Kasimir Malevich's paintings point to a subversive expansion of the concept of aesthetic purity beyond the bounds of a proto-Kantian disinterestedness.

Malevich may be the first artist for whom form, color, surface, and composition exist in the purposiveness of pure relations as presentations freed from objectivity for "something supersensible." Each work is characterized by a supplementarity which makes it possible to collide abstraction and figuration, elements of one work with another, even to the point of backdating works painted decades earlier. This aesthetic supplementarity points to a realm of aesthetic purity, a primacy of pure feeling which he names "suprematism." Despite bold variations in composition and color, the suprematist form of an "objectless world" frees the work from a dialectic which reconciles subject and object.

Malevich concedes that an aesthetic presentation is never completely formed but is always in a discontinuous state of transformation, in accordance with other presentations which invariably surface as collisions in imaginal difference. In turn, each work of art is embedded in the purposive form of imagination, notably the pure work of art that is formed ever anew in the compelling contributions of diverse aesthetic possibilities.

One of his early oil paintings, *Bathing Women* (1908), points to the distinguishing features of an unbroken *aesthetic interplay* between the pure work of art set up by imaginal judgment and particular presentations of artworks. The primacy of the pure play of form suggests that no work of art is present solely in what is perceived to be the compositional structure of an art object. On the contrary, there is no work of art given completely to itself. What we have is a suprematist mirroring of visual forms and imaginal presentations. Through this mirroring, the artwork is released from a determinate reflection of its material structure, so that it may be judged according to the imaginal play of purposiveness. Malevich's painting conveys the primacy of this play by highlighting the ephemeral white figures, who appear ready to step out of the painting. One is presented, it seems, with an apparition within the aesthetic presentation of the visual configurations of colors. The "ecstasis" of the bathing women is suprematist even though the work is figurative. On closer view, one of the figures in fact walks toward a blue-colored stream into the opaque scene of the painting. Yet, all three of the white figures signify the transitory presence of a pure work of art in the compositional play of sensations. While Malevich's *Bathing Women* exhibits the difference between a suprematist and representational presentation, it also marks the new aesthetic "identity" of play and surface. What withdraws from the work is drawn into the work of art. In a manner of speaking, the figures present their withdrawal as purposive play to imagination, which, nonetheless, returns the abstraction to figuration so that the pure work of art is always already engaged in play with a particular art work. Whether we are dealing with the early or the late works of Malevich, the artist or the theorist of art, we cannot separate the suprematist from the figurative paintings, unless we are willing to part with his supplementary theory of art.

It seems to me that this theory amplifies Kant's aesthetics of purity. It shows that the aesthetic dimension consists in manners of presentation which generously enlarge the presentational powers of the cognitive forces on the basis of imagination's relation to individual works of art. Most of Malevich's paintings reveal his commitment to the primacy of pure sensation. His work extends Kant's discussion of aesthetic judgment into the domain of painting. More importantly, however, Malevich's theory of suprematist art exposes a distinctive aesthetic schema which relates judgment to art without subsuming art under judgment. Such a relation reveals abstract and figurative images of an "objectless world" beyond time, in a free place called the work of art. Judgment, then, is challenged by an art that is rid of the ballast of the object. What can be extracted from presentations of individual works is the chance of countless different exposures to artworks in general. Such a wealth of aesthetic exposure is possible only if the relation between judgment and art remains disinterested, universal, purposive, and necessary. In short, the *aesthetic* relation must be free. See Charlotte Douglas' fine article on Malevich, "Behind the Suprematist Mirror," in *Art in America* (September 1989), 164–77.

CHAPTER 7. RADICAL SPACING IN 'GELASSENHEIT'

1. Compare Michel Foucault's "Nietzsche, Genealogy, History," trans. Donald Bouchard and Sherry Simon, in *The Foucault Reader* (New York: Pantheon Books, 1984), 87.
2. "Heidegger focuses on the way in which a certain kind of image functions within

such comportment, an image sighted in advance, the anticipated look [*das vorweggenommene Aussehen*] of the thing to be produced" (John Sallis, in "Imagination and the meaning of Being", 130). Capital alludes to the anticipatory seeing within filming, but not from the perspective of image. In one sense, one can say capital seizes the image; it lets the image fall silently.

3. Filming is related to the matter of "phenomenon" as it is explored by Heidegger in *Sein und Zeit*. The difference between filming and Heidegger's understanding of "phenomenon" lies in the dimension of reason's divergence (*Entfernung*) from the ontological mood of reflection. Filming transposes Heidegger's insight of "showing" into a "reflective" mirroring, without the ontological intensity of presence which still marks his phenomenological orientation. Silently, filming glides along the imaginary wall of being, blurring the ontological difference. Yet, Heidegger's path of thinking guides our reflections on filming, particularly Heidegger's allusions to *Gelassenheit*. There thinking exceeds the presence of being. And filming reveals the Apollinian turn to imagination's "free play." The composure of reason (*Gelassenheit*) makes filming as *physis* of our epoch possible. Its sign may be read but does not demand to be read. Thus, there is a sense in which Heidegger's understanding of *phainesthai* already broaches filming. The aim of "phenomenon" converges with the turn of filming from metaphysics to the disseminative composure of reason. Indeed, the Heideggerian text points to a distinctive showing of *Denken*, a "sigetics" that filming carries to its radical conclusion beyond the postmodern scene.

Filming is also a "showing" but not a "self-showing" or a "bringing to light" of presence. There is no nostalgic-ontologic dimension in the post-phenomenological emergence of "phainesthai" as filming. Filming may be regarded as an "appearing," yet, neither in the transcendental-subjective (Kantian) sense nor in the ontological (early Heideggerian) sense of "showing-in-itself." Something distinctive occurs in filming: a kind of thinking that fades from the "showing" of presence without fading from "showing." The notion of presence still determines the Kantian and the Heideggerian concepts of "showing." In critical philosophy, for example, we are challenged by the very presence of the transcendental subject; in the early Heidegger's phenomenology, we are overwhelmed by the presence of Being. Filming, on the other hand, ruptures Heidegger's phenomenological concept of phenomenon. Although it retains a sense of what Heidegger calls, in respect of phenomenon, "a distinctive way something can be encountered" (*SZ*, 41), filming no longer encounters being. It exceeds the "light" of essence, what Heidegger defines as "the *transcendens* pure and simple." This does not make filming everything. On the contrary, filming merely ex-poses what is granted in the velocity of the postmodern scene. Hence, it shows capital in its reflective *kinesis*, in its nonidentical dispersion, in its phenomenal dissemination. Filming perhaps signifies a radical historical re-marking of Spinoza's fifteenth proposition in book one of the *Ethics*. Marked differently, the proposition would then read: "Everything that exists, exists in capital, and nothing can be or be conceived of without capital." Spinoza's own statement is, of course: "Quicquid est, in Deo est, et nihil sine Deo esse neque concipi potest": *Opera Quotquot Reperta Sunt*, recognoverunt J. Van Vloten et J. P. N. Land (The Hague: Martinus Nijhoff, 1914), 47. Filming indicates this distinctive unfolding of human history. It does not confirm capital per se; indeed, it deconstructs the dialectic priority of capital as substance or essence of history. Capital, therefore, does not emerge as the last referent, but rather as a former signified fading into a reflective movement of imagination. In the power of imagination's new terrain, capital signifies a "clearing" within filming. It emerges as the velocity of history in imagination.

4. For an illuminating theory of Kant's understanding of freedom, see Bernard Carnois, *The Coherence of Kant's Doctrine of Freedom*, trans. David Booth (Chicago: University of Chicago Press, 1987).

5. *Geist/Gelassenheit* opens the entire analysis of the relation of capital and filming.

6. Although filming, as it is named in this text, diverges from Heidegger's thought in general, it implies the proximity of *Gelassenheit* developed by Heidegger in *Gelassenheit* (Pfullingen: Verlag Günther Neske, 1985), particularly on the basis of his statement: "Wir ahnen das Wesen des Denkens als Gelassenheit" ("We surmise the essence of thinking as letting-go") (52).

7. Sallis articulates such a texture with regard to "spacing": "Reiterated lapse, almost without limit; slippage into the open, spreading truth even into untruth" (*S*, ix).

8. The promise of capital, which the beautiful-in-nature signifies, remains sporadic and uncertain. "Like every promise, the beautiful in nature is feeble in that it is just a promise" (*AT*, 108).

9. Cf. Sallis, *Spacings*, 113.

10. "Die Abgeschiedenheit west als der lautere Geist" ("Apartness abides as disinterested spirit": my translation). Martin Heidegger, *Unterwegs zur Sprache* (Frankfurt am Main: Vittorio Klostermann, 1985), 62.

11. It seems that Foucault's genealogy is still an "archaeology of the self." Filming is a more complex disruption of the subject. See Foucault's *Le Souci de Soi* (*Histoire de la Sexualité*, 3) (Paris: Editions Gallimard, 1984), 53–85.

12. Compare Deleuze's reference to Goethe's theory of light in *Cinema 1*, 93.

13. A detailed and rewarding study critical of "the Hollywood tyranny of images" is Timothy Corrigan's *The Films of Werner Herzog (Between Mirage and History)* (New York and London: Methuen, 1986). For another illuminating study of this theme, see Eric Rentschler, *German Film and Literature* (New York and London: Methuen, 1986).

CHAPTER 8. SURFLECTANTS—STRIFE OF FILMIC SURFACES

1. "For, in order to express what is ineffable in the mental state accompanying a certain presentation and to make it universally communicable—whether the expression consists in language or painting or plastic art—we need an ability [viz., spirit] to appehend the imagination's rapidly passing play and to unite it in a concept that can be communicated without the constraint of rules (a concept that on that very account is original, while at the same time it reveals a new rule that could not have been inferred from any earlier principles or examples)" (*CJ*, 186).

2. One of the modes of capital's sublime speaking can be discerned in relation to music. Our use of the term music as *mousike*, however, is quite different from the cultural phenomenon of music per se. *Mousike*, that is, filming's incision into imagination, paves the way for a disruptive space of postmodern judgment. In short, *mousike* may be regarded as the "last metaphysical instance" of an ethical disposition, a postmodern mood that is related to the apparition of natural beauty. *Mousike* is the art of searching after the felling of ground. Only from

that perspective may art or filming be called "musical." Although the ethical referent is eclipsed by the discursive dehiscence of metaphysics, filming is not without an *ethos* in the sublime post-homelessness of subjectivity. *Mousike* emerges as the discursive *ethos* of capital. It is, of course, not a particular musical phenomenon, which determines the interval of capital between imaging and filming, but rather *mousike* in the disseminal mode of imagination's rhythm. In short, *mousike* is the yearning (*Sehnsucht*) of discourse, invariably deprived of a founding *telos*, intimately bound up with a filmic hearing. This hearing involves a more radical listening, which withdraws from being as it crystallizes a new turn toward capital and its apparitional discourse. Here it is important to note that apparition is not filmic nihilism. It does not empty capital of its movement or its surflectants. Instead, it is closely related to *mousike*, perhaps the only ethical modality of capital that surfaces in discourse. Apparition, then, leaves intact a unique dis-position (*ethos*), a filming outside appearances: a luminous swaying of music and discourse. This swaying, which subverts the independence of music from language, occurs in the nameless terrain of imagination's radical play of "tectonic," by virtue of which capital is consistently something other than what it has been conceived to be in the history of theory and practice.

Not contingent upon a historical manifestation of music, imagination's tectonic is aligned with "shattered instants" of a disembodied musical phenomenon, a rhythm-in-exile which is not dominated by universal technology. Briefly stated, Bruckner's symphonic language provides an avenue of entry into this tectonic. For one, his *adagio* progressions seem to arrest the sublime movement of capital by unfolding freely from tonal digressions, through intense chromaticism, to the nonoriginary, nonidentical momentary stillness of E major. Disrupting the aesthetic spell of identity, Bruckner refuses to deliver melodic moments to a *retournons* of dialectical unity. The aesthetic tension revealed in the mood of D minor in the first movement of Bruckner's Ninth Symphony is never released; it remains a nonidentity, an indication that spirit is not yet at home in the free and open region of imagination. For now we are bracketing the problem of music's empirical or effective communication of capital, which is daily replicated in contemporary popular music. What we wish to do here is merely glance at "instants" of filming, i.e., sublime traces of capital which expose musically dispersed, mimetically disruptive moments of *Sehnsucht* ("longing") without presence. In brief, *mousike* relates to a mood which effaces ground, to a feeling without a will for moral, political, or transcendental configurations of pleasure and displeasure. Music passes through the spacings of capital, a roaming, "erring" *ethos*, if you will, of imagination's postmodern play. It is not "there" to give comfort for the absence of the political or social. Indeed, it is not there at all except as post-aesthetic power of withdrawal. In turn, filming is disengaged from teleologic reappropriations, while music announces its fissures, its sigetic surflectants, which resist narrowly framed socio-cultural perceptions. In the end, music supplements the com-posure of discourse heard through the filmic art of surflection. Reserving a site for filming's itinerary, music opens imagination's nonidentical spacings of capital, ever yielding new passages of discourse, showing, most of all, a filmic displacement of *Sehnsucht*. By supplementing the "discursive textuality" of filming, music spontaneously arrests *Bewegung* ("movement"), as Bruckner's symphonies indicate. No attempt is made to recapture transcendence or to regain subjectivity or any other metaphysical investment in this fleeting instant. What occurs is a convergence of imagination and *Denken*. The power of filmic surflectants, in the form of musical moments, radicalizes capital's genealogy by tracing the path of imagination's sublime subversion of imaging. As one voice of the sublime, music deflects the reflective cascade of capital from theoretical and practical presence.

3. *Auctoritas* denotes "decision" and "power." The *auctoritas* of filming, however, inscribes a disembodied, musical mood into the "power" of capital.

4. "Sigetic," derived from the Gr. *sigan* (not-saying), refers to the *other* beginning of thought which filming explores. See Martin Heidegger's attempts to found a "sigetics" (*Sigetik*) in his *Beiträge zur Philosophie* (*Vom Ereignis*) (Frankfurt am Main: Vittorio Klostermann, 1989, 78).

5. To cite Fichte: "It is impossible to reflect without having abstracted." See *Fichtes Werke*, ed. I. H. Fichte (Berlin: Walter de Gruyter, 1971), I:72.

CHAPTER 9. FILMING—A POSTMODERN MODE OF JUDGMENT

1. Gabriel Garcia Marquez describes a postmodern upheaval in a literary sense: "One could hear the neat destruction of ninety thousand, five hundred champagne glasses breaking, one after the other, from stem to stem, and then, the light came out and it was no longer a March dawn but the noon of a radiant Wednesday" ("Monologue of Isabel Watching It Rain in Macondo," in *Leafstorm and other Stories*, trans. G. Rabassa [New York: Harper & Row, 1972], 120).

2. Cf. Luce Irigaray, *Speculum of the Other Woman*, trans. G. C. Gill (Ithaca, N. Y.: Cornell University Press, 1989), 13–129.

3. To the extent that Heidegger's concept of *Ge-stell* appears to be "the essential glance of being" (*der Wesensblick des Seins*), it can be said to prefigure, as does his earlier allusion to *phainesthai*, what comes into view, insofar as judgment looks away, over, and beyond the principle of ground. According to Heidegger, the essence of technology lies in the object's fading from the presence of subject to a presencing (*Bestand*) of *Ge-stell*. *Bestand—bestehen* names technology's distinctive presence, a going through, a standing in the clearing. A new coming to presence emerges, a shining-showing of being that is marked *Gefahr*. While the correct translation for *Gefahr* is "danger," Heidegger's use of this term is more complex. *Gefahr* is also the name for "being-at-play," as one may be at play in a race track, as one may lose one's life in such play. *Fahren* means to fare, sail, travel, drive, and *Ge* is an old usage for "go," "get ahead," "leave." Thus, a double sense of "going" and "forward" is inscribed in *Gefahr*, a paradoxical "destination" of being. The *Gefahr* of the essence of technology lies in being's turn from the privilege of presence to a shining-showing of presencing. In short, *Ereignis* is established as *Eräugnis*. And the clearing of being comes to presence as "filming," a showing of the essence of truth from the perspective of enframing. Heidegger does not articulate what permeates the turn of being from *presence* to *Bestand*, a technological presencing whose participatory movement of *aletheia* is still a mimetic enterprise. *Bestand*, it seems, is a necessary showing (but not the only showing) of the *Offenständigkeit* of being. Between man and the gods, the earth and the sky lies the *Offenständigkeit* of being of which presencing (*Bestand*) is merely a passing through. Presencing, therefore, is not entirely free from the privilege of presence. At most, it appears to be a mimetic fading of presence. But as long as *mimesis* determines thinking in its new task,

the echo of philosophy will be heard again and again. A horizon of metaphysics will prevail upon thinking until a withdrawal from the illusion of the originary takes place. The *Fragestellung* of being must, therefore, be turned from a *mimesis* of a primal coming to presencing. From Plato's *eidos* to technology's *Ge-stell*, being comes to presence as the ordaining of a mimetic destining. Heidegger's search for a "genuine *a priori*" reveals a historical, albeit not logocentric, prioritizing of *mimesis* of being. He still understands presencing as an ontological event of *mimesis*. The matter of thinking, then, belongs to being-in-*mimesis*. In the end, this mimetic impulse toward the originary reveals a technology which comes to presence as *Ge-stell*.

While Heidegger does not name "filming" per se, he announces filming in being's coming to presence as *Ge-stell*, that is to say, in "brightness playing in the open" (*BW*, 383). Still, filming persists in questioning the truth of being in a more disruptive mode than Heidegger's "step back." It attempts to undertake the *Fragestellung* ("questioning") of being in a terrain free of *mimesis*, while it questions the "unheard voice" of being which echoes in the history of metaphysics. But, by the same token, being is here regarded as freely at play with *Ge-stell*, and the essence of technology as capital is not read as danger, according to ordinary usage, but as *Rettung* ("saving-power") from *mimesis*, the actual, metaphysical danger of thinking. From Platonism to its inversion in Nietzsche's philosophy of the will to power and Adorno's unique advance into an aesthetics of redemption, *mimesis* persists as ground of reflection. In Heidegger's final phase of the turn in being from *Gefahr* to *Rettung*, there is a sense of brightness that begins to illuminate an initial effacement of *mimesis*.

Conversely, filming films away *mimesis*. It does not even belong to capital. What it illuminates is the apparition of capital: the beauty of a shining-showing of free doing (*Verhältnis*). Filming has no pretensions to be philosophical. And still, it cannot be thought to be outside the problematic of the relation between philosophy and non-philosophy. It turns away from metaphysics not because it has found a new immediacy of thought. There is neither immediacy nor mediation of reflection in filming in a mimetological, metaphysical sense.

How can filming unmask the *mimesis* of philosophy? Does not non-philosophy begin in imitation of philosophy? It seems that filming is neither philosophy nor non-philosophy. It would be absurd to view it as nonphilosophical; this would still confine it to the philosophical terrain. For to speak of non-philosophy is to speak philosophically. Is there no thinking that exceeds philosophy? Even science, which does not think in the sense philosophy does, is rooted in philosophy. Heidegger claims that thinking and philosophy are not necessarily one and the same, and that a radical turn within the genealogy of being invites a mode of thinking that "breaks open the territory" of metaphysics. Being as *Ge-stell* may still be thought mimetically; nonetheless, *Ge-stell* announces a coming to presence that is different from metaphysical presence. What begins to be illuminated here is what filming projects: a mode of thinking which consistently questions the privilege of a discourse on philosophy and non-philosophy in order to let thinking be, and in order to let imagination play in the open epoch of judgment's sigetic.

4. *Ur-teil* is meant to convey a "primal difference," "an originary part" of *Denken*, a first cut from totality, an epoch of distinct particularity, a judging that is peculiar to filming.

A "geneafilmic" inquiry is one which discerns both the family (*genea*) resemblances of the dialectic covering or "filming" of being gripped in rationality (*logos*), and the filming which unveils this covering. Consequently, a "geneafilmic" approach is more radically aware of the substantive dominance of the principle of ground in the history of philosophy than a "genealogical" procedure.

EXERGUE: FASSBINDER, HERZOG, AND 'BRIGHTNESS PLAYING'

1. Cf. Stanley Cavell, *The World Viewed* (Cambridge, Mass.: Harvard University Press, 1979), 102.
2. The condition of filmmaking is not unrelated to that of western philosophy today, assuming the following is true: "Western philosophy seems to have exhausted its capacity to produce a new vision of reality" (Joan Stambaugh, *The Real Is not the Rational* [Albany, N. Y.: State University of New York Press, 1986], ix).
3. Walter Benjamin alludes to this event from a socio-cultural perspective with his concept of "mechanical reproduction." See "The Work of Art in the Age of Mechanical Reproduction," in Walter Benjamin, *Illuminations*, ed. Hannah Arendt (New York: Schocken Books, 1969).
4. From the final scene of *Despair*, Fassbinder's first English-language film of 1978, based on the Vladimir Nabokov novel. The German subtitle of the film is *Eine Reise ins Licht* (*Journey into the Light*). The screenplay was written by Tom Stoppard.
5. "Ich bin von allem abgetan" uttered by Kaspar Hauser in the midst of Prof. Daumer's attempt to deprive his innocent student of a counterstructural mode of viewing the world, in Werner Herzog's film *The Enigma of Kaspar Hauser* (West Germany: ZDF-TV, 1975).
6. *Ästhetische Theorie* (Franfurt am Main: Suhrkamp, 1980), 100.
7. Compare Wim Wenders' *Falsche Bewegung* (*Wrong Move*, 1974), a film which underscores the facility of indulging in "false movements."
8. Rothman, "Vertigo: The Unknown Woman in Hitchcock," in *The "I" of the Camera* (Cambridge: Cambridge University Press, 1988), 152–73.
9. Irigaray, *Speculum of the other Woman*, 238.
10. See Elizabeth Frank, "Art's Off-the-Wall Critic," *The New York Times Magazine*, Sec. 6 (November 19, 1989): 46. While Danto in his "end-of-art theory" appears to argue for art's *Kehre* toward philosophy as an indiscernible turn within the domain of reflection, filming consists in the dissolution of philosophy through a post-aesthetic, that is, a discernible turn to an "indiscernible" mode of judging (*Ur-teil*).
11. Conversation between Madeleine and Scottie in Hitchcock's *Vertigo*, 1958.
12. In German *filmen* means to film, to make a film . The verb *filmen* most closely approximates the gerund "filming," particularly with regard to its open and non-completing "movement" of judgment.
13. Compare Mark C. Taylor, *Altarity* (Chicago: University of Chicago Press, 1987).
14. Filming's turn is an approaching and a receding from Heidegger's thought.
15. Compare Jacques Derrida, *De l'esprit* (Paris: Editions Galilee, 1987).
16. See Siegfried Kracauer, *From Caligari to Hitler* (Princeton: Princeton University Press, 1974), 297–307.
17. Theodor Adorno, *Minima Moralia*, trans. E. F. N. Jephcott (London: NLB, 1974), 247.

Glossary

◆

AB-GRUND (abyss). Word used by Heidegger to deconstruct the metaphysical concept of ground. In a Nietzschean manner, Heidegger invites a hovering over the abyss, a freeing from the *principle* of ground. Both a rooted and rootless understanding of ground.

ALETHEIA (truth). The essence of truth, which unveils being. Heidegger's point of focus exceeds a representational sense of truth. *A-letheia* signifies truth as simple unconcealment, illuminating a counter-dialectic opening for thought.

APPARITION. Word used by Adorno in order to convey an "aesthetic," epistemic rupture of appearances. It is used here as a detonation of the imaginal, thereby installing a gap in imagination's withdrawal from essencing. Derived from *ap-pareo*, "to appear," "to show," "apparition" shows what cannot be seen, the absence of epistemic modes of presencing.

AUCTORITAS. Not a political category. Dis-position of "imagination" without being. A perception of power without presence, a disembodied mood of *Ansehen* (appearing). A non-necessitarian mode of judgment (decision-power).

BEURTEILUNG (discernment). Kant's word for a distinctive mode of judging the beautiful and the sublime. Exceeds representational operations of judgment (*Urteil*).

BEWEGGRUND. Ordinarily, "motive or reason for action." Otherwise, the name for an opening of ground, lit. "moving ground."

BEWEGUNG (movement). Thinking on the way to filming. A continual disrupting of a political *Beweggrund*, such as *die Bewegung* of the 1930s. Imagination's mode of exceeding its imaginal being.

CAPITAL. Apparition of ground, beauty of filming. Linked to what is not yet, the possible, a nonimaginal scene. Subversive consequence of filmic explosion of rationality.

DASEIN. Lit. "presence," "existence," "being here." Heidegger's name for "being-in-the-world," existing primarily in being-with-others. As "Being-possible" (*Seinkönnen*), *Dasein* radically displaces the metaphysics of the subject.

DENKEN (thinking). A path of "reflection" in the face of the end of metaphysics. Philosophy's "other beginning" of thinking language in relation to being.

DAWNING. Spirit's free opening of filming, exposing a teleologic, photo-ontic fall of imagination.

DE-LIGHTING. Withdrawing from the *phaos* (light) of being and its *Schein*, or dialectic illusion. Casts a shadow upon metaphysical masks of reflection as well as postmodern imageries of transgression.

DIFFERENCE. (1) Removed from its customary usage, the word denotes a sense of departure from the principle of identity celebrated in German Idealism. (2) A post-conceptual understanding of difference, particularly in Heidegger's disclosure of the ontological division between being and beings. (3) A Derridean play of the trace, invariably otherwise than difference.

ÉCRITURE (writing). A Derridean mode of thought that weaves and interlaces the continuous and discontinuous motifs of philosophy's farewell. An old name for what is unthought in what has always been called writing.

EINBILDUNGSKRAFT (imagination). (1) The aesthetic power of freeing imagination from the epistemological closure of metaphysics. Kant's sense of imaginal "free play," whereby thinking understands imagination in its openness. (2) A "postmodern" change of terrain in which filming begins to break with the teleologic concerns of transcendental imagination.

ERÄUGNIS. Derived from the archaic verb *eräugnen*, "to bring to one's eyes," "to bring to light." In Heidegger's text, *Eräugnis* serves to underscore a distinctive ontological seeing of the "essence" of technology. A prefilmic naming of filming.

EREIGNISSE. Adorno's own naming of the aesthetic subversion within art works. Non-events of de-lighting political presence. Works of art straying toward an "appearing that does not exist" (*AT*, 121).

FILMEN. Ger. "to film." An imaginal showing of judgment's turn from political blindspots. Ontic de-light in filming.

FILMING. Name for a site of thinking in this epoch. Uncovers limited and limiting shining of metaphysical and postmodern reflection. Implosive sighting of postmodern strife. Fissuring of imaginal "thinking."

"FILMING." An illusory seeing or coating of being/beings.

GEFAHR (the danger). Heidegger proposes an ontological reading of danger in relation to the essence of technology. The journey (*Fahren*) of being in the experience (*Erfahrung*) of technology.

GEIST (spirit). (1) Metaphysical representation of the absolute. (2) A site of thinking in which judgment withdraws from the dialectic principle of identity.

GEIST/GELASSENHEIT. Spirit free of *Geist* as absolute form of self consciousness. A filmic denuding of *mimesis*.

GELASSENHEIT (letting go). A favored word of Johann Eckhart (and Heidegger), which denotes a sense of reaching beyond representational thinking. A freeing of thinking for *das Fünklein* (*scintilla*), "the spark" of a radical opening. Used here to designate a disjunctive, non-necessary terrain of judgment. *Gelassenheit* is here translated as "com-posure" in order to highlight a sense of *componere* in filming's operation of "putting together," "constellating" what is severed or fractured in the realm of judgment. "Com-posure" is also related to *pausare*, "to stop," "pause," in the sense of casting a "pause" on filming in order to drive out (*urgere*) the film in "filming."

GE-STELL (enframing). The essence of the technological epoch. Not to be regarded in a positive or negative sense.

GLISSEMENT (sliding). (1) A new epistemic locus of knowledge which reveals a fading from the centered ego. (2) A sliding away from ground. A falling into the abyss of a post-aesthetic filming.

HEIMAT. (1) Feeling at home. The site of the identity of subject. Images of nearness and nature. A fundamental concept of German romanticism. (2) A socio-political narrowing of the principle of ground—the *Heimat* movement under national socialism. (3) For Heidegger, the truth revealed through language. (4) More recently, in leftist German literature, the homeland of the child, the innocence of life without fear.

KEHRE. (turning). Heidegger's naming of a deepening of the ontological enterprise toward *Gelassenheit*. With regard to filming, *Kehre* marks a turning from imagination's "free play" to the open terrain of the sublime gap in judging (*Ur-teil*).

LICHTUNG (clearing). Primordial shining of being. An ontological opening in which truth is revealed through language. Filming's post-metaphysical beginning.

MIMESIS (imitation). (1) The basis for an aesthetic rationality. (2) An ideal of art exceeding the principle of identity. An aesthetic modification of the vertical Platonic structure of *mimesis*. (3) A desire for a literature of judging free of practical and theoretical interests.

DAS NATURSCHÖNE (the-beautiful-in-nature). (1) In Kant's aesthetics, the formal condition for imagination's "free play." (2) In Adorno's *Aesthetic Theory*, the "central motif" of art, continually challenging the infrastructural closure of society. (3) Awakens thought to the phenomenal variants of a radically different mode of judging.

PHAINESTHAI. Used by Heidegger to underscore a singular way of apprehending something. A self-showing of what appears. Used here in the sense of a shining without essencing, without an ontologic constraint, yet with regard to a "shining-through" the masking and "filming" of beings.

PRINCIPIUM RATIONIS SUFFICIENTIS (the principle of sufficient reason). Fundamental principle of metaphysics and the sciences. A system of concepts, a totality of connected ideas in a unique dialectic terrain that consolidates reason and being.

The certitude of an ultimate explanation.

PROMESSE DU BONHEUR (promise of happiness). An aesthetic hope for a counter-tendency to reification.

SEHNSUCHT (longing). (1) A romanticist desire to turn the curve of reason into a circle of imagination. (2) A radical mode of judging the curve of imagination far from the center.

SIGETICS. Derived from the Greek *sigan*, "to be silent." In questioning power (*Fragekraft*), sigetics, for Heidegger, is simultaneously, paradoxically, the pre- and post-aesthetic beginning of thinking. Reveals poetic power of the word. *Originary* thinking, philosophy's *other* beginning.

THEA (the look). Advancing a new "look" of judgment falling from the order of ground to the abyss of filming.

UR-TEIL. A "primal" severing (*teilen*) of imagination (*Einbildungskraft*) from the power of rationality in order to prepare for a filmic constellation of *Geist* and *Gelassenheit*.

ZERISSENHEIT (rupture). Breaking the alliance of being and ground, time (*Zeit*) and spirit (*Geist*). *Dasein* thrown into apartness.

Bibliography

◆

Adorno, Theodor W. *Aesthetic Theory*, trans. C. Lenhardt. London and New York: Routledge & Kegan Paul, 1984.
———. *Ästhetische Theorie*. Frankfurt am Main: Suhrkamp, 1970.
———. *Kierkegaard, Construction of the Aesthetic*, trans. R. Hullot-Kentor. Minneapolis: University of Minnesota Press, 1989.
———. *Minima Moralia*, trans. E. F. N. Jephcott. London: NLB, 1974.
———. *Philosophische Frühschriften, Gesammelte Schriften*, Vol. 1. Frankfurt am Main: Suhrkamp, 1973.
———. *Prisms*, trans. S. and S. Weber. Cambridge, Mass.: The MIT Press, 1981.
———. *In Search of Wagner*, trans. R. Livingstone. Manchester: NLB Press, 1981.
———. *Vermischte Schriften, Gesammelte Schriften*, Vol. 20 (1–2). Frankfurt am Main: Suhrkamp, 1986.
———. and Eisler, Hanns. *Komposition für den Film, Gesammelte Schriften*, Vol. 15. Frankfurt am Main: Suhrkamp, 1976.

Arnheim, Rudolf. *Film as Art*. Berkeley: University of California Press, 1957.

Auerbach, Erich. *Mimesis*, trans. W. R. Trask. Princeton, N. J.: Princeton University Press, 1953.

Avisar, Ilan. *Screening the Holocaust: Cinema's Images of the Unimaginable*. Bloomington: Indiana University Press, 1988.

Balázs, Béla. *Theory of the Film*, trans. E. Bone. New York: Dover, 1970.

Barthes, Roland. *Image/Music/Text*, trans. Stephen Heath. New York: Hill & Wang, 1977.
———. *Camera Lucida*, trans. Richard Howard. New York: Hill & Wang, 1981.

Baudelaire, Charles. *Les Fleurs du Mal*, trans. Richard Howard. Boston: David R. Godine, 1983.

Baudrillard, Jean. *The Mirror of Production*, trans. Mark Poster. St. Louis: Telos, 1975.

Benjamin, Walter. *Illuminations*, trans. H. Arendt. New York: Schocken Books, 1969.
———. *Reflections*, trans. E. Jephcott. New York and London: Harcourt Brace Jovanovich, 1978.

Bergmann, Peter. *Nietzsche, "the Last Antipolitical German."* Bloomington: Indiana University Press, 1987.

Bernasconi, Robert. *The Question of Language in Heidegger's History of Being.* Atlantic Highlands, NJ: Humanities Press International, 1985.

Biemel, Walter. *Die Bedeutung von Kants Begründung der Ästhetik für die Philosophie der Kunst.* Köln: Kölner Universitäts Verlag, 1959.

Bloch, Ernst. *Das Prinzip der Hoffnung.* Frankfurt: Suhrkamp, 1959.

Boeder, Heribert. *Das Vernunft-Gefüge der Moderne.* Freiburg: Verlag Karl Alber, 1988.

Bourdieu, Pierre. *Distinction: A Social Critique of the Judgment of Taste,* trans. Richard Nice. Cambridge, Mass.: Harvard University Press, 1984.

Bruns, Gerald L. *Heidegger's Estrangements.* New Haven and London: Yale University Press, 1989.

Bürger, Peter. *Theory of the Avant-Garde,* trans. Michael Shaw. Minneapolis: University of Minnesota Press, 1984.

Casey, S. Edward. *Imagining: A Phenomenological Study.* Bloomington: Indiana University Press, 1976.

Caputo, John. *Radical Hermeneutics: Repetition, Deconstruction, and the Hermeneutic Project.* Bloomington: Indiana University Press, 1987.

Carnois, Bernard. *The Coherence of Kant's Doctrine of Freedom,* trans. D. Booth. Chicago: University of Chicago Press, 1987.

Cavell, Stanley. *The World Viewed.* Cambridge, Mass.: Harvard University Press, 1979.

Corrigan, Timothy. *The Displaced Image.* Austin: University of Texas Press, 1983.
———. (Ed.) *The Films of Werner Herzog.* New York and London: Methuen, 1986.

Dallmayr, Fred R. *Twilight of Subjectivity.* Amherst: MIT Press, 1983.

Danto, Arthur. *The Transfiguration of the Commonplace.* Cambridge, Mass.: Harvard University Press, 1981.

Deleuze, Gilles. *Cinéma 1, L'image-mouvement.* Paris: Les editions de minuit, 1983.
———. *Cinéma 2, Time-Image.* Minneapolis: University of Minnesota Press, 1989.

Derrida, Jacques. *Dissemination,* trans. Barbara Johnson. Chicago: University of Chicago Press, 1981.
———. *De l'esprit.* Paris: Editions Galilee, 1987.
———. *Of Grammatology,* trans. G. Spivak. Baltimore: Johns Hopkins University Press, 1976.
———. *Margins of Philosophy,* trans. A. Bass. Chicago: University of Chicago Press, 1982.
———. *Positions,* trans. A. Bass. Chicago: University of Chicago Press, 1981.
———. *The Truth in Painting,* trans. G. Bennington and I. Mcleod. Chicago: University of Chicago Press, 1987.

Eagleton, Terry. *Against the Grain*. London: Verso, NLB, 1986.

Ecker, Gisela. (Ed.) *Feminist Aesthetics*, trans. H. Anderson. Boston: Beacon Press, 1985.

Eco, Umberto. *Travels in Hyperreality*. New York: Harcourt Brace Jovanovich, 1986.

Eisner, Lotte H. *The Haunted Screen*, trans. Roger Greaves. Berkeley: University of California Press, 1973.

Ellis, John M. *The Theory of Literary Criticism*. Berkeley: University Press, 1974.

Eucken, Rudolf. *Geschichte der Philosophischen Terminologie*. Leipzig, 1879.

Faden, Gerhard. *Der Schein der Kunst*: *Zu Heideggers Kritik der Ästhetik*. Würzburg: Konigshausen-Neumann, 1986.

Fichte, I. H. (Ed.) *Fichtes Werke*. Berlin: Walter de Gruyter, 1971.

Fichte, Johann Gottlieb. *The Science of Knowledge*, trans. P. Heath and J. Lachs. Cambridge: Cambridge University Press, 1982.

Fink, Eugen. *Sein, Wahrheit, Welt*. The Hague: Martinus Nijhoff, 1958.

Foster, Hal. (Ed.) *The Anti-Aesthetic*. Port Townsend, Washington: Bay Press, 1983.

Foucault, Michel. *The History of Sexuality*, Volume I: *An Introduction*. New York: Vintage, 1980.
———. *The Order of Things*, trans. A. Sheridan-Smith. New York: Random House, 1970.
———. *Le Souci de Soi (Histoire de la Sexualité*, 3). Paris: Editions Gallimard, 1984.

Fynsk, Christopher. *Heidegger: Thought and Historicity*. Ithaca: Cornell University Press, 1986.

Gadamer, Hans-Georg. *Wahrheit und Methode*. Tübingen: J. C. B. Mohr, 1972.

Ortega y Gasset, Jose. *Velázquez, Goya and the Dehumanization of Art*, trans. A. Brown. New York: W. W. Norton & Co., 1972.

Gasché, Rodolphe. *The Tain of the Mirror*. Cambridge, Mass.: Harvard University Press, 1986.

Gilligan, Carol. *In a Different Voice*. Cambridge, Mass.: Harvard University Press, 1982.

Greenberg, Clement. *Art and Culture*. Boston: Beacon Press, 1961.

Habermas, Jürgen. *The Philosophical Discourse of Modernity*, trans. F. Lawrence. Cambridge, Mass.: MIT Press, 1987.

Halliburton, David. *Poetic Thinking: An Approach to Heidegger*. Chicago: University of Chicago Press, 1981.

Hall, David L. *Eros and Irony*, Albany: SUNY Press, 1982.

Hartman, Geoffrey H. *Criticism in the Wilderness*. New Haven & London: Yale University Press, 1980.

————. *Saving the Text*: *Literature/Derrida/Philosophy*. Baltimore and London: The Johns Hopkins University Press, 1981.

Haug, W. F. *Critique of Commodity Aesthetics*, trans. Robert Bock. Minneapolis: University of Minnesota Press, 1986.

Hegel, Georg Wilhelm Friedrich. *Phänomenologie des Geistes*. Frankfurt am Main: Suhrkamp, 1970.

Heidegger, Martin, *Basic Writings*, trans. D. F. Krell. New York: Harper & Row, 1977.
————. *Beiträge zur Philosophie (Vom Ereignis)*. Frankfurt am Main: Vittorio Klostermann, 1989.
————. *Aus der Erfahrung des Denkens (1910–1976)*. Frankfurt am Main: Vittorio Klostermann, 1983.
————. *Gelassenheit*. Pfullingen: Verlag Günther Neske, 1985.
————. *The Question concerning Technology and Other Essays*, trans. W. Lovitt. New York: Harper & Row, 1977.
————. *Sein und Zeit*. Tübingen: Max Niemeyer, 1967.
————. *Die Technik und die Kehre*. Pfullingen: Verlag Günther Neske, 1962.
————. *Wegmarken*. Frankfurt am Main: Vittorio Klostermann, 1976.

Herrmann, Friedrich Wilhelm von. *Die Selbstinterpretation Martin Heideggers*. Meisenheim am Glan: Verlag Anton Hain, 1964.

Hölderlin, Friedrich. *Poems and Fragments*, trans. M. Hamburger. Ann Arbor: University of Michigan Press, 1968.
————. *Sämtliche Werke*, ed. Friedrich Beissner, Vol. 3. Stuttgart: W. Kohlhammer Verlag, 1957.

Husserl, Edmund. *Phantasie, Bildbewusstsein, Erinnerung*. The Hague: Martinus Nijhoff, 1980.

Irigaray, Luce. *Speculum of the other Woman*, trans. G. C. Gill. Ithaca, N.Y.: Cornell University Press, 1989.

Jameson, Fredric, *Marxism and Form*. Princeton: Princeton University Press, 1971.

Jay, Martin. *Adorno*. Cambridge, Mass.: Harvard University Press, 1984.

Judovitz, Dalia. *Subjectivity and Representation: The Origin of Modern Thought in Descartes*. Cambridge: Cambridge University Press, 1987.

Kaes, Anton, *From Hitler to Heimat*. Cambridge, Mass. and London: Harvard University Press, 1989.

Kant, Immanuel. *Critique of Judgment*, trans. W. S. Pluhar. Indianapolis: Hackett, 1987.
————. *Critique of Pure Reason*, trans. N. K. Smith. New York: St. Martin's Press. 1965.
————. *Kritik der Urteilskraft*. Frankfurt am Main: Suhrkamp, 1974.

Kellner, Douglas. *Herbert Marcuse and the Crisis of Marxism*. Berkeley: University of California Press, 1984.

Kelly, Douglas. *Medieval Imagination*. Madison: University of Wisconsin Press, 1978.

Kochler, Hans. *Skepsis und Gesellschaftskritik im Denken Martin Heideggers.* Meisenheim am Glan: Verlag Anton Hain, 1976.

Kockelmanns, Joseph. *Heidegger on Art and Artworks.* Dordrecht: Martinus Nijhoff, 1985.

Kolb, David. *The Critique of Pure Modernity.* Chicago: University of Chicago Press, 1987.

Kracauer, Siegfried. *Theory of Film.* New York: Oxford University Press, 1960.
———. *From Caligari to Hitler.* Princeton: Princeton University Press, 1974.

Krell, David Farrell. *Intimations of Mortality: Time, Truth, and Finitude in Heidegger's Thinking of Being.* State College: Pennsylvania State University Press, 1986.

Kroker, Arthur, and Cook, David. *The Postmodern Scene.* New York: St. Martin Press, 1986.

Leitch, Vincent B. *Deconstructive Criticism.* New York: Columbia University Press, 1983.

Lacan, Jacques. *The Language of the Self*, trans. A. Wilden. Baltimore: Johns Hopkins Press, 1968.

Lentricchia, Frank. *After the New Criticism.* Chicago: University of Chicago Press, 1980.

Levin, David Michael. *The Body's Recollection of Being.* London: Routledge and Kegan Paul, 1985.

Linares, Filadelfo. *Der Philosoph und die Politik.* Meisenheim am Glan: Verlag Anton Hain, 1972.

Lyotard, Jean-Francois. *La condition postmoderne: rapport sur le savoir.* Paris: Les editions de minuit, 1979.

Marcuse, Herbert. *Eros and Civilization.* Boston: Beacon Press, 1966.

Marx, Karl, and Engels, Friedrich, *Collected Works.* New York: International Publishers, 1975–84.
———. *Das Kapital.* Vol. 3. Berlin: Dietz Verlag, 1957.

McCumber, John. *Poetic Interaction.* Chicago: University of Chicago Press, 1989.

Megill, Allan. *Prophets of Extremity: Nietzsche, Heidegger, Foucault, Derrida.* Berkeley and Los Angeles: University of California Press, 1985.

Metz, Christian, *The Imaginary Signifier*, trans. C. Britton, A. Williams, B. Brewster, A. Guzzetti. Bloomington: Indiana University Press, 1982.

Miller, J. Hillis. *The Linguistic Moment: From Wordsworth to Stevens.* Princeton: Princeton University Press, 1985.

Morchen, Hermann. *Die Einbildungskraft bei Kant.* Tübingen: Max Niemeyer Verlag, 1970.
———. *Adorno und Heidegger: Untersuchungen einer philosophischen Kommunikationsverweigerung.* Stuttgart: Klett-Cotta, 1981.

Nehamas, Alexander. *Nietzsche*: *Life as Literature*. Cambridge Mass.: Harvard University Press, 1985.

Nichols, Bill. *Ideology and the Image*. Bloomington: Indiana University Press, 1981.

Nietzsche, Friedrich. *Beyond Good and Evil*, trans. W. Kaufmann. New York: Random House, 1966.
———. *Thus Spoke Zarathustra*, in *The Portable Nietzsche*, trans. W. Kaufmann. New York: Viking Press, 1968.
———. *Vom Nutzen und Nachteil der Historie für das Leben*. München: Carl Hanser, 1966.
———. *Werke*: *Kritische Gesamtausgabe*, ed. G. Colli and M. Montinari. Circa 30 vols. Berlin: Walter de Gruyter, 1967—.
———. *The Will to Power*, trans. W. Kaufmann and R. J. Hollingdale. New York: Vintage, 1968.

Pöggeler, Otto. *Der Denkweg Martin Heideggers*. Pfullingen: Neske, 1963.

Rentschler, Eric. *German Film and Literature*. New York and London: Methuen, 1986.

Ricoeur, Paul. *The Rule of Metaphor*, trans. R. Czerny, et al. Toronto: University of Toronto Press, 1977.

Rorty, Richard. *Contingency, Irony, and Solidarity*. New York: Cambridge University Press, 1989.

Sallis, John. *The Gathering of Reason*. Athens: Ohio University Press, 1980.
———. *Spacings—of Reason and Imagination*. Chicago: University of Chicago Press, 1987.

Sartre, Jean-Paul. *Imagination*. Ann Arbor: University of Michigan Press, 1972.

Schelling, Friedrich Wilhelm Joseph. *System of Transcendental Idealism*, trans. P. Heath. Charlottesville: University Press of Virginia, 1978.

Schott, Robin May. *Cognition and Eros*. Boston: Beacon Press, 1988.

Shapiro, Gary. *Nietzschean Narratives*. Bloomington: Indiana University Press, 1989.

Silverman, Hugh J. *Inscriptions*: *Between Phenomenology and Structuralism*. New York and London: Routledge & Kegan Paul, 1987.

Schmidt, Dennis J. *The Ubiquity of the Finite*. Cambridge, Mass.: The MIT Press, 1988.

Schmidt, Gerhard. *Vom Wesen der Aussage*. Meisenheim am Glan: Verlag Anton Hain, 1956.

Schurmann, Rainer. *Heidegger on Being and Acting*: *From Principles to Anarchy*, trans. C.-M. Gros. Bloomington: Indiana University Press, 1987.

Scott, Charles E. *The Language of Difference*. Atlantic Highlands, N. J.: Humanities Press, 1987.

Smith, Paul. *The Historian and Film*. Cambridge: Cambridge University Press, 1976.

Sontag, Susan. *On Photography*. New York: Penguin, 1977.

Spinoza, Benedicti de. *Opera Quotquot Reperta Sunt*, ed. J. V. Vloten and J. P. N. Land. *Opera* 1–2. The Hague: Martinus Nijhoff, 1919.

Stambaugh, Joan. *The Real Is not the Rational*. Albany, N.Y.: SUNY Press, 1986.

Struve, Wolfgang. *Philosophie und Transzendenz*. Freiburg: Verlag Rombach, 1969.

Taminiaux, Jacques, *La Nostalgie de la Grece a l'aube de l'idealisme Allemand*. The Hague: Matinus Nijhoff, 1967.

Taylor, Mark C. *Altarity*. Chicago: University of Chicago Press, 1987.

Trakl, Georg. *Das dichterische Werk*. München: Deutscher Taschenbuch Verlag, 1972.

Unger, Roberto Mangabeira. *False Necessity*. Cambridge: Cambridge University Press, 1987.

Waldenfels, Bernhard. *Das Sokratische Fragen*. Meisenheim am Glan: Verlag Anton Hain, 1961.

Wenders, Wim. *Emotion Pictures: Essays und Filmkritiken*. Frankfurt am Main: Verlag der Autoren, 1986.

Wurzer, Wilhelm S. *Nietzsche und Spinoza*. Meisenheim am Glan: Verlag Anton Hain, 1975.

Index

◆